Faces of
FINDHORN

Faces of FINDHORN
Images of a Planetary Family

by THE FINDHORN COMMUNITY

1817

HARPER & ROW, PUBLISHERS, New York
Cambridge, Hagerstown, Philadelphia, San Francisco,
London, Mexico City, São Paulo, Sydney

Compiled and Edited by **Edwin Maynard**

Unless otherwise indicated, all quotes by David Spangler are from talks shared with the Findhorn Community between 1970 and 1973. © 1973 Findhorn Foundation.

"Findhorn: Garden or Jungle," by Myrtle Glines, is based on an article of the same title originally published in the *New Age Journal* and *United Focus Journal,* © 1974 Myrtle Glines.

Dorothy Maclean's quote and Deva messages are from her book *To Hear the Angels Sing,* published by Findhorn Publications, © 1980 Dorothy Maclean.

Celtic drawings copyright © 1979 by Alice Rigan.

Photographs copyright © 1980 by The Findhorn Foundation except as follows:

Pages 13, 21, 22, 23, 40, 42 bottom, 62 top, 64 top, 69, 90 top, 91, 102, 112–113, 118, 123 top, 128, 130 bottom, 136, 140, 143, 144, 150, 167 top left and bottom, copyright © 1980 by Kathy Thormod.

Pages 3, 14 top right, 25, 36 top, 44–45, 46, 48, 49, 61 top, 64 bottom, 70 bottom, 80, 82, 87, 88 top right, 95 top, 97 top, 100–101, 147, 158 top, 166 top, 168, 175 top, copyright © 1980 by Edwin Maynard.

Pages 15 top, 32 bottom, 34, 59, 65 top right, 66–67, 76 bottom, 79 right, 86 top, 88 top left, 98 top, 99 bottom left, 134 left, 162, 163, copyright © 1980 by Jerry Howard.

Pages 117, 119, 121 bottom, 122 left, copyright © 1980 by Margaret Fuller.

Pages 50, 51, 132, 133, 161, copyright © 1980 by Gary Elliot Burke.

Pages 26, 42, copyright © 1980 by Rowena Pattee.

Pages 36 third from top, 61 right, copyright © 1980 by Terry Killam.

Page 98 left, copyright © 1980 by Michael van der Ley.

Page 171 bottom right, copyright © 1980 by The Cosanti Foundation.

Page 173 top, copyright © 1980 by Daniel Brown.

Photographic editing by **Kathy Thormod**

FIRST EDITION

LIBRARY OF CONGRESS CATALOG CARD NUMBER: 78-20160
ISBN: 0-06-011268-9
ISBN: 0-06-090851-3 pbk.

80 81 82 83 84 10 9 8 7 6 5 4 3 2 1

Design by **Linda Morris**

Acknowledgments

Compiled and Edited by Edwin Maynard
Photographic Editing by Kathy Thormod
Design by Linda Morris

Photographs by Kathy Thormod, Edwin Maynard and Jerry Howard. Additional photographs by Charles Petersen, Margaret Fuller, Will Elwell, Gary Elliot Burke, Marion Stoker, Simon Bell, Eric Müller, Rowena Pattee, Terry Killam, Robert Vente, Crispin Currant, Kathleen Fekete, Rennie Innis, Angus Marland, Rod Thompson, Stephen Clark, Edward Paul, Richard Valeriano, Annie Worth, Michael van der Ley, Steve Beck, Ivan Pinter, Daniel Brown and Denny Ferry.

*Cover design, calligraphy
and artwork by* Linda Morris

Cartoons by Aidan Meehan

Erraid map and Celtic artwork by Alice Rigan

Typeset in Palatino by John Hewer, Edinburgh

Grateful acknowledgements go to Rue Wallace for her vital contribution in getting this book under way; to Liza Schnadt for compiling and editing Peter and Eileen's chapter; to David McNamara and Marianna Lines who worked together on "Relationship and Community"; and to Tom Buchan, Ralph White, Jeremy Slocombe and Dennis Evenson, whose help extended far beyond the individual sections they contributed. Thanks also to 'Stan' Stanfield, David Platts, David McNamara, Charles Petersen and Frances Edwards for their invaluable assistance in checking the text and helping to shape this book into a whole. Special thanks also to Paul Piehler and Paul Hawken for their constructive criticism, and to David Spangler and Myrtle Glines not only for their written contributions but for their trust, encouragement and true friendship. Thanks to Kathy Thormod, Toya Blagojevitch and Michael Lunt for their help with the design; to Elaine Rose Gardner for her valuable contribution in the final preparation of the layouts; and to Gareth Rostoker for his meticulous care with the graphic darkroom work.

Our appreciation also goes to Marianna Lines, Marion Stoker and Mary Stanton for their aid in coordinating the transcription of tapes and the typing of manuscripts; without their dedication and patience it would never have been possible to complete a book authored by an entire community. We'd also like to express our thanks to the many working guests at Findhorn who shared their typing skills when extra hands were needed.

Many others from outside Findhorn have also contributed generously. We would particularly like to express our appreciation to Marjorie Bair, Wendy Lewis and Susan Kedgley for their editorial assistance.

Final thanks go to Buz Wyeth and Steve Roos of Harper & Row for their sustaining trust and support; and, of course, to the entire Findhorn community, without whose manifold help and cooperation this book would never have come into being.

Our work is dedicated in thanksgiving to all the visible and invisible helpers with whom we share in the co-creation of a new Earth.

For more information about the Findhorn Foundation and its activities please write to: Findhorn Foundation, The Park, Forres, SCOTLAND IV 36 OTZ.

David Spangler

Findhorn and the Vision
of a Planetary Culture

Afterword

Myrtle Glines

Findhorn: Garden or Jungle?

Tom Buchan

From the Ground Up

Ralph White

Politics and Synergy
The Network of Light

Contents

Jeremy Slocombe

Manifestation, Finance, and
Right Livelihood

Dennis Evenson

Messengers from Within

Foreword

Findhorn is a complex and diverse place to live, and the problems and dynamics confronted there are as pressing and often as poignant as the ones we all face in our own communities, neighborhoods and homes. Like the gardens that surround the community, Findhorn must constantly deal with the varied and diverse forces which constitute life itself.

Where human beings attempt to act as one group and also encourage individuality, there will be conflict, differences and, inevitably, personal change. Oftentimes the search for community is the search for a haven of certainty and homogeneity where our neighbors all spell God with a small *g*. In a world where chaos, disorder and sheer irrationality are growing, it is a natural impulse for us to seek a life less surprising, a future more secure, and a reality more reassuring than the ones we find on the front pages. What Findhorn reveals is that such certainty and homogeneity are a luxury we can ill afford.

The increasing differentiation and conflict in the world is not an imperative to jump for the belief system that comes along, but is rather a plea for everyone to understand the many selves within them and the many souls about us. This is what Findhorn is attempting. For if there is ever to be anything remotely resembling a "New Age," it will come about because people have learned to deal with their differences in ways that nurture, encourage and support life, not because we have suppressed our differences in favor of a new belief system. It will come about because we will, with those differences, transform our lives in place, in daily action, in our jobs and in our neighborhoods. Such a transformation will not come about by abandoning our homes and searching for it "out there." If one thinks that Findhorn may be that place "out there," this book reveals the common thread of humanity that runs through our lives, whoever and wherever we are. Findhorn is not a place to sequester our fears, nor is it a place where generous platitudes can replace social interaction. More than any other community I've visited, Findhorn deals head on with the full spectrum of human diversity; and it is in Findhorn's search for tolerance, acceptance and receptivity that I find hope for a better world.

Faces of Findhorn is not meant to entice us to Scotland, or diminish who we are at home. Rather, and I quote Camus, it is to remind us that there are human beings everywhere "whose deeds and work every day negate the crudest implications of history. As a result, there shines forth fleetingly the ever-threatened truth that each and every being, on the foundations of their own suffering and joy, builds for all."

Paul G. Hawken

Palo Alto, March 25, 1980

ix

1 Vision

I thought I was coming to Findhorn
to learn from initiates how to make my way along the path
without the stumbling I seemed prone to.
What I found were extraordinary people
with barked shins and scraped knees just like mine, who were
struggling earnestly and with great strength to understand,
from the inside out, a consciousness and a vision which says,
"Humankind is holy. Everything is unity."
People at Findhorn have as many questions and probably
no more answers than anyone else.
Or rather, we do have answers: in our hearts, a
creative vision of the harmony and wholeness of life; in our
minds, the whole spectrum of spiritual principles to use as tools
and guides; and a very special place in which to experience
the outworking of the answers. But living here, living
anywhere, is a moment-by-moment adventure in fashioning meaning
from myth and theory by doing whatever one is doing.
That, for me, is the hub of it all – the day-to-day hard work
of real life as a mystical experience.
Rue

... the life impulse that we all share, the dream of humanity that will reach the stars, not in spaceships, but in life and consciousness,

that humanity is arising, and one aspect of its birth is a place like Findhorn.

This is a book of images. In it we find the faces of a highly diverse group of people whose common link is a sharing of the Findhorn experience. Looking at them, we may ask what has drawn these people together from their different walks of life. Such a question also leads us to questions about Findhorn itself: Why does such a place exist? What prompts people, often at considerable personal sacrifice, to come here to visit or to live? Why has it become, often unwittingly, a focal point for glamor and myth, until its reality competes with its legend, and the community itself must struggle to be free of the expectations of our utopian longings?

Many factors have fed Findhorn's growth, both as a place and as an image. They range from the spirit of adventure and of new beginnings, to the desire for transformation, and the need for places where inspiration can flow from positive, creative efforts to build an enlightened and joyful human future. Yet one idea, more than any other, represents the seed from which Findhorn and all that it has created has sprung. It is the idea that a planetary culture is emerging in our time and that places like Findhorn exist to explore, to serve, and to further that emergence.

Many people think of Findhorn as if it were an isolated expression. They know there are communities springing up around the world, but they feel that what we are doing at Findhorn and in other communities, we are doing by ourselves, as if it were a retreat away from society and its problems. They are not aware of what is becoming a worldwide transformation, and that individuals in every country of this world and every walk of life are pursuing essentially the same vision.

# of a Planetary Culture   *by David Spangler*

When I was at university studying molecular biology, one of the interesting areas that was developing was the process known as "cloning". Cloning is based on the realization that within every human being is a chemical essence of that person on a physical level. Every cell, no matter how differentiated – a liver cell or a spleen cell – has exactly the same chromosomal makeup; in theory one can take a cell from a person and literally grow that person all over again, and in so doing he or she will be almost an exact physical duplicate of the original. Within us, then, even on the cellular level, there exists a vision of what we are. On the spiritual level, humankind has a similar integral vision, and all that we are and have been and shall ever be is the outgrowth of that integral spiritual pattern, that seed dream which may well have its flowering beyond this planet altogether.

Within each of us and within us collectively, this dream lives and seeks release. Ultimately, no individuals are so conditioned by their environment that there does not exist within them, to be tapped and used at will and discretion, a life force, an energy which can transcend their environment.

Once when I was living in a small town, the city council decided to widen the main roadway. The old roadway had a row of trees running down its middle, and the planners decided that the trees had to go to make way for progress; so out came the trees, and in their place was put a concrete island dividing the lanes of traffic. What they forgot to do was to uproot the trees, and about three months after the road was completed it began to crack. It split open as the growing stumps pushed their way back through the slabs of concrete and asphalt that had been laid over them.

I am sure the city council only saw it as a lesson in how not to build a road; but it is a classic example of the power of the life force as it reaches to externalize, to actualize its ever-present vision.

To penetrate to its underlying vision, while living in earthly form, is humanity's challenge. Like the concrete that is spread over the road and trees, man's cultures tend to crystallize and ossify, and then the life force has to burst its way through again. It cannot be resisted.

Now, after centuries of working in this rather energy-wasting fashion of building things up, letting them get stale and hard, then having to break through them, we stand at the threshold of having developed enough awareness that humanity shares a transcendent potential, and that perhaps we can learn to build a society and live a life attuned to its essence. This is the challenge of our time: to enter into a new consciousness which can, in turn, give birth to a new world.

The vision of an emergent planetary culture involves the broadening and deepening of our individual and collective perspectives and assumptions so that we embrace ourselves as a species, as humankind, rather than as separate factions. It involves, moreover, seeing ourselves as sensitive, interdependent members of a community of life that transcends the human and embraces the whole of planetary ecology, including the Earth itself as a living being. It is not seeing ourselves only as Eastern or Western, American, British, Russian, Chinese, African, or Asian. It is the rediscovery of our shared species identity that unites us beyond our national, racial, religious, economic and political boundaries.

Within this broadened context, our current different cultures can still exist. They are simply deepened to touch our human roots, not just our

1

ethnic ones; they are expanded to embrace our planetary existence and our ecological interdependence rather than being confined to parochial interests. Monoculture ultimately spells stagnation and death. What we are evolving is a context strong enough and deep enough to encourage the creative richness of diversity in the same way that life itself expresses its infinite variety of potential.

Anyone who moves into such a consciousness is stepping into a New Age. It doesn't matter whether they are living at Findhorn or whether they be anarchist, Baptist or Buddhist. If they seek to serve humanity in a way that we know inwardly will help the potential of humankind emerge, then essentially they have a grasp of what the New Age is.

Humanity, as a whole, is passing through a tremendous period of self-examination brought on, among other things, by man's recent discovery of the power of ultimate planetary destruction. So humanity is taking stock and saying, "How can I rule a world filled with animal instincts, greed, hatred and separation? How can I handle these immense powers?"

Atomic power is nothing compared to the power of the dream that lives in each of us that is seeking emergence. How are we to handle godliness if we cannot handle our personalities? Godliness is where we are headed. Nothing less will suffice for the life that is within us. Our personalities are consciousness bound and determined by form; godliness is consciousness boundless and self-determining through its awareness of the essential life that links all of us, all of nature, and even the furthest stars. Today, throughout the world, millions of people are consciously working with this vision.

People who have this vision of humanity unfolding its divinity are bringing that vision about in different ways; but more and more they are learning that all these ways involve both going within to work on oneself and expressing oneself in an increasingly inclusive fashion. Those who are doing so are starting centers, groups, communities and cooperative networks throughout the world. One doesn't have to talk about the New Age to be part of it; but the life impulse that we all share, the dream of humanity that will reach the stars, not in spaceships, but in life and in consciousness, *that* humanity is arising, and one aspect of its birth is a place like Findhorn.

The New Age is not for some people to create and others to watch. We are all participants. There would be no such things as spectators in a nuclear war; and there can be no such thing as a spectator upon this planet now. We are all participating in very vital ways, if only through our thoughts and emotions; and we cannot underestimate the power of thoughts and emotions, even in the seclusion of our homes, to affect what Jung called the "collective unconscious", the collective myths that make up the mind and heart of the planet.

We are all storytellers, mythmakers: our lives, our thoughts, feelings, dreams, desires and self-images are tales that we project to the world. Like the stories that ancient men and women told around campfires and in sacred places, our myths give definition, meaning, order and significance to our personal realities. Cultures are like stories, too. They are tales told by some part of humanity about what it means to be human, to live on this Earth, to strive, to rejoice, to feel pain, to sorrow, to be born, to die, to triumph and to transcend.

The function of a planetary culture and the role within it of places like Findhorn is the creation of a spiritual, psychic and psychological condition, a "meta-linguistic" condition of connectedness, which allows people to tell their stories to each other with communication and not conflict, so that in the telling we may all begin to hear and see the greater stories that our species and our planet have been trying to share for thousands of years. The story of human destiny must now open a new chapter and become a story of planetary destiny and unfoldment as well.

Above all else, Findhorn is a place where the stories of Earth may gather to be told and heard. These are more than the stories of all the individuals in this book and the hundreds of others who are not represented here except in spirit; they are more than the stories of the various cultural backgrounds that meet in this spiritual community. They are stories, not only of human desires and vision, meaning and significance, but also of the longings and visions of the Earth itself – stories of other kingdoms and other forms of life that share this world with us, stories of nature, of the cosmos and of deeper levels of creation. In such a gathering of stories, our context, our culture, is enlarged, until we can learn to speak the meta-language of creation in symbols of love and wholeness.

Ultimately, Findhorn is a place of communication, from which communion and community may develop. This is what a planetary culture is, too; the matrix from which a true planetary communion and community may emerge, not simply a world government or economy. In our time we are learning to stop telling our own tales so urgently and insistently and to listen again to our world. It is Findhorn's role to be a microcosm of this exchange; a place of listening, of sharing, of communication and community.

People come to Findhorn because somewhere, sometime in their lives they have heard the deeper, more ancient, more promising tales of our planetary culture. They have heard its language behind their own, its vision within their own, and they seek a place to share their stories in new ways, in ways that reveal rather than conceal the inner reality. They seek a place to listen and a place where they may be listened to more deeply than is usual in our society. In so doing they are becoming images and image-makers of a new culture, which is also, in its essential roots, the oldest and only culture there has ever been.

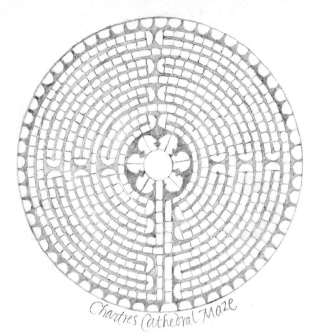
Chartres Cathedral Maze

11 Experience

There is a design on the floor of Chartres Cathedral
that symbolizes the intricacies of evolutionary growth.
The symbol consists of a maze whose center can be approached
directly as you enter. At first it seems that
you will penetrate immediately to the center of the maze.
However, as the pattern is traced at Chartres, you cannot
actually enter the center before you turn and encounter
every little nook and cranny of the maze.
In a similar way, we must integrate our insight with every
aspect of human life before returning, finally,
to the center of our being and completing, at that moment,
the sacred process of initiation.
Milenko

From the Ground Up

T*om:* 3 a.m. Pineridge. A midsummer's day. Sunrise is already tipping the pine trees with pink and gold. A gull flies silently in the high clear sky. I sit with the beginnings of this chapter and a strong cup of coffee. Outside a black cat emerges from the undergrowth, looks around and yawns: pink mouth. A baby in the next caravan is crying for the breast. Morning emptiness inside the skull experiences sounds and colors and beings for themselves without interior commentary.

I like to write at this time of the morning even during the dark winter months. It's the time when I get most of my work done – in silence and, particularly with poetry, in a sort of crystalline hypnagogic state between dream and waking. I cannot type during this period for fear of waking my son, Lewis, through the frail partitions of our caravan trailer. So I write in longhand.

I doze off around seven and am reawakened by Lewis' friend Mark who lives across the road with his parents and grandparents. He has called to see that Lewis is up and ready for school in the nearby town of Forres.

8:20. Scattered groups of people have passed, mostly on foot, on their way to morning meditation in the sanctuary. Others are now leaving on foot or by bicycle or motorcycle for their morning "attunements" with their work groups. "Woodstock", the big blue double-decker bus arriving from Cluny Hill, will have already disgorged up to sixty members and guests for a day's activity in the many work departments at Findhorn.

Mark Lerner, one of our resident astrologers, whizzes past with a carload of diaper buckets in

Aerial view of the Park

his little red Honda with California plates. Leona and Dieter leave, like a pair of tousle-haired twins, in their ancient bottle-green Volkswagen: Dieter, who is German, to work as a stone mason with the construction crew and Leona, a Canadian, to the Androgyny Workshop she is giving five miles away at Newbold House in Forres.

The day is now quite hot. I leave the doors and windows of the caravan open and walk down towards the center of the community, pausing to enjoy my garden, which is a mass of long grass, dandelions, celandines, poppies, wild trefoils

8   **Jeremy:** *Part of my networking job, linking with other new age groups, communities and individuals around the world, has been to computerize our filing systems. Our files are growing so fast that this is the only way we can keep up. At the moment a letter can come in saying: "Please send me a list of spiritual communities and centers in southern Europe," and it takes too long to go through the cards manually and reply to all the similar letters with specific requests that are coming in at the same time.*

Shortly after I started the networking job I had a recurring dream about "Apple", our computer. In the dead of night I would get out of bed and sneak down to the room in which it is housed in the bowels of the Universal Hall, and sit down and attune with the machine and type on the keyboard, "Apple, are you ready to make contact?" Each time the computer would reply, "Syntax Error," which is its way of saying it doesn't understand. Night after night, in my dream, I sneaked down and typed, "Apple, are you ready to make contact?" Then one night the single word "Yes" appeared on the screen.

From then on, before doing any work with "Apple", I would sit down with it and attune to the intelligence that lay beyond the machine, the consciousness behind its physical form. I found that the contact was powerful and came remarkably easy. My learning about the workings of the computer came from that rather than from the manual I'd been laboring to understand.

and heathers. Pineridge itself has something of the feel of a frontier town in contrast to the more suburban center of the trailer park. In winter, when it would be dark still at this time of day, the air would be fragrant with wood smoke; today the sea of yellow gorse over the nearby sand dunes fills the air with a scent like incense.

Outside the Universal Hall, and again by the potting shed and compost heaps in the central gardens, I pass circles of working groups, members and guests holding hands in a ring with their eyes closed for a few moments of silent attunement.

I arrive early for an editorial meeting. While we're waiting, Jeremy and I exchange notes on our dream lives, and Jeremy tells me of a series of dreams he's had that have totally changed his working relationship with "Apple", the community computer.

After a brief meditation we continue with the almost interminable process of trying to write, design and edit a book as a group. Such meetings can go on for hours and can talk themselves into circles – particularly editorial meetings in which one is often talking about words. It can seem a terrible way to write a book, but it's a great education. The endlessness of the process, whatever else it may be, is a constant reminder that one's real work is not so much in the external activity as in a kind of inner attentiveness that is going on all the time.

I usually feel completely whacked at the end of an editorial meeting, as if I had done a day's work in two or three hours. I stop in the Publications building to do some photocopying. It's a warm day. Everyone is in shorts; many are barefooted. The radio plays softly; the dozen or so people in the room have their heads down working. Bruvver, a huge white cat, lies in the sun. All the windows are open. I love the feeling of a lot of hard work being done in a totally relaxed atmosphere.

I spend the rest of the morning working in the new vegetable gardens in a five-acre field by Cullerne, an old Scottish house the community has recently bought half-a-mile down the road between the caravan park and Findhorn village.

We're tilling the soil by hand, digging through a thin layer of turf to sand, shale, and what used to be beach stones, removing the couch grass and putting manure down to the depth where roots will need it. Although the work is back-breaking, there is a powerful connectedness which comes from the sense of helping build and deepen the soil.

Before lunch a busload of hot and dusty people from the community drives down the dirt road to the beach, where they swim and skim Frisbees in the icy waters of the Moray Firth.

Lunchtime itself is the hub of the social day. The lawn outside the Community Center is strewn with brightly clothed people of all ages and nationalities, all eating the vegetarian fare and talking in the sunlight. People are rushing about, tripping over children, eating, making contact, exchanging information like bees at the center of the hive.

After lunch I wander up to Reception to collect my mail and then go on to meet the afternoon tour at the grocery store which the community runs for the owner of the site. Although the caravan park may look like the most inappropriate setting imaginable for a new age community, there are not many other locations in which a community like this could have grown to such a size so unobtrusively. However, a clear and open relationship with our neighbors is very

important to us, and we have tours every day to show our neighbors and many visitors around the whole community, so that they can see for themselves what we're up to.

I swap banter with Roy and Muriel, two fellow Scots who are running the shop. Muriel is at the counter and her irrepressible laughter ripples around the shelves. We joke about life on the £5-a-week member's allowance.

Muriel: *We have a little bit of money of our own. We have always kept some money back. At one point we were going to give everything to the community; then we realized that would make us dependent, and we wouldn't be able to run a car. We felt we needed to be independent, and the car is useful for going into town, to collect things for the shop, and just to get away from the community at times – that seems important.*

At 2:00 I muster the tour. I never know who I'll get: suspicious Scots full of questions about the community's finances; an American minister or two guarded against our esotericism; several curious tourists who are here to see the gardens; and the odd backpacker expecting to see devas or nature spirits behind every bush. At the height of our summer season we can have over fifty visitors a day, but today there are only a dozen or so.

First we go to the Community Center where I give a brief outline of the origins of the community: how Peter and Eileen Caddy and Dorothy Maclean's long years of spiritual training had led them to Cluny Hill Hotel where Peter was manager; how their actions were directed by guidance from the voice of the God within; how, despite trebling the hotel's business and raising it from a three- to a four-star rating within five years, Peter was suddenly transferred to another hotel without warning and then given the sack; how the three of them, together with Peter and Eileen's three boys, were led by Eileen's guidance to live for the next seven years in a small caravan next to a rubbish dump on the edge of the sand dunes in the trailer park near Findhorn; how, in accordance with the guidance they received, they set about establishing a small garden in the sand and scrub; and how, to the astonishment of experts, their results were phenomenal, producing plants whose variety and vigor could not be conventionally explained. It was finally revealed that the garden's extraordinary growth resulted from a unique experiment in conscious cooperation between humanity and nature, based on Peter's intuition, Eileen's guidance, and the contact of Dorothy Maclean with the Deva (or archetypal intelligence) of each plant species.

As the garden began to attract worldwide attention, others were drawn to this nucleus and there evolved, in this unlikely caravan park setting, a thriving spiritual community of over three hundred people.

Many are already familiar with this part of the story. What is harder to describe is the way the community has been learning to cope with the challenges that fame has brought. After a flood of articles and books and a movie about Findhorn in the mid-seventies, the community was faced with a growing influx of visitors, and responded with the development of its educational programs and a phase of rapid expansion. We have greatly benefited from the support and encouragement we have received for the continuation of our work, but at the same time we have been creaking at the seams with the strains of accelerated growth.

In five years we have moved from the original cluster of caravans and prefabricated houses into a community of groups living in a dozen different places. We are fast becoming a group of small communities, and are still evolving the internal structures to adapt as an organism.

For a number of years it was easy for community members to sit back and feel vicariously important because of all the attention coming to Findhorn, without their always seeing the necessity of creating the magic for themselves. However, the community as a whole seems to have been moving through a rite of passage from adolescence to maturity. There's been an increasing realization that the real work, which is only beginning, is not just to establish this one community but to help establish a network of Light, or a critical mass, if you will, of many thousands of individuals, groups and communities which together can transform this planet.

12

In talking of the network of Light I am invariably reminded of the story of the monkey on an island colony who one day got the idea of washing the mud off sweet potatoes before eating them. Soon most of the colony had learned the trick until, say, ninety-nine monkeys were doing it. Then one day, the hundredth monkey picked up the knack, and simultaneously, on several other islands, for the first time monkeys started to wash their food. Lyall Watson, who recounts this story, believes that the transformative power of myth spreads through human societies in the same kind of way.

We do a lot of collective thinking, probably more than any other social species, although it goes on in something like secrecy. We don't acknowledge the gift publicly, and we are not as celebrated as the insects, but we do it. Effortlessly, without giving it a moment's thought, we are capable of changing our language, music, manners, morals, entertainment, even the way we dress, all around the earth in a year's turning. We seem to do this by general agreement, without voting or even polling. We simply think our way along, pass information around, exchange codes disguised as art, change our minds, transform ourselves.

Lewis Thomas
The Lives of a Cell

We leave the Community Center and go outside into the bright sunlight, through the gardens – whose smallness often surprises people – the Sanctuary, the Communications Center, the Universal Hall, the publications building, the craft studios in Pineridge, and back towards the store. Always new questions to stop and consider, or familiar ones to deal with afresh.

TOM: Living in the community you have lots of people to relate to, instead of just your parents. What's that like?

AMBER: *It's fun.*

RUBY: *Like Louise. I invited her to the community on Open Day. And when she came she said, "You're lucky to have all these things here." I didn't realize that before, because I'm used to it. Like having the playground; and you know everyone's names; and you can be funny with everyone and just be friends with everyone, and things. Sometimes the village kids call us Caddys. They take all the bus seats and say, "Don't let the Caddys have any," or, "The next stop is the Caddys'."*

TOM: What are some of the things you do in the community?

RUBY: *We help cook or work in publications sometimes. In the children's program we went for picnics and walks in the woods, and did things with clay and painted pictures. We had a sanctuary in the children's pavilion.*

TOM: What did you do in the sanctuary?

RUBY: *In the morning, just meditate. Sit in a circle and close our eyes.*

TOM: If you were trying to tell someone who didn't know about meditation what it was, what would you say?

RUBY: *Tuning in to God.*

TOM: What's that mean?

AMBER: *You ask God things.*

TOM: What do you say?

RUBY: *You don't have to say anything. He just understands what you think. Don't you know how to meditate? You just close your eyes and be silent.*

As I'm walking home after the tour I meet Ruby and Amber lolloping home from school like a couple of naughty, cuddly kittens.

"Hullo, Haggis," says Amber. She is smoking a candy cigarette.

Ruby is ten and Amber is eight. They attend the local primary school in Kinloss. I ask them if the kids are any different there.

RUBY: *Not very different. They bring different food – more sweets – and they swear all the time.*

On my way back to Pineridge I pause and look across the barley field to the airbase half-a-mile away. Nimrods are taking off to go on patrol over the North Atlantic, Phantoms taking off in twos and fours, their afterburners glowing pink even in the sunlight. Noises of the airbase are always there in the background of our life at Findhorn, like rumbles of thunder, as a reminder of the different realities that impinge on us constantly.

Back home I sort through a pile of tape transcripts to piece into the mosaic of this book. All around me are folders full of manuscripts, letters, scribbled lists and statistics, together with transcripts of the dreams, reflections, opinions and personal fables of a whole community. The theme that emerges consistently through all this material is the struggle to ground a visionary life in everyday experience.

I pick out two interviews to edit. The first is with Elsie, an elderly member of the community. The second is with Liza, a thirty-year-old South African friend who, like so many others, stumbled unwittingly on this nondescript caravan park and stayed.

Elsie: *I first came here with my husband eleven years ago. Eileen's guidance was what drew us to Findhorn. There was something from the very first page of her book,* God Spoke to Me, *that struck home.*

It took us a year to make the move. My daughter and friends thought we were mad to up and leave everything at our age, but that didn't put us off, and we got here in the end. Then my husband died when we'd been in the community only a few weeks. My daughter and all our friends in Cornwall said, "Well, of course you'll come back with us now, won't you?" Yet that was further from my mind than ever. I knew that this was where I should be, although there was nothing

here then but the sanctuary, the garden, Peter and Eileen's caravan, and one or two bungalows.

Sometimes I feel a bit dismayed at the way things are moving, at the loss of the intimacy we had when the community was small, or at the rate of the community's expansion. But I accepted it from the beginning because, you see, Eileen's guidance has always said that we would grow from a family, to a village and then to a city of Light.

The transitions haven't been easy and we've made our share of mistakes as a community. So our passage has been stormy at times. It could never be completely peaceful here, and I'm glad of that. I wouldn't want that sort of static perfection. But there can always be inner peace; that's what drew me here, and that's what keeps me here still.

Liza: *One of the major challenges Findhorn has come through in the last five years is in learning to work from the ground up with the emotional and personality aspects of community members' lives. Many of these aspects were suppressed or denied during the early days when people were trying to live purely from the visionary level on which the community was founded.*

When I came in 1974, it was work, work, work, except on Sundays or on particularly hot days in summer when everyone would drop everything, pile into buses and go hiking in the mountains. The energy level was very high, and a lot of music came out of that time. But what also happened with all that cooperation and love was that people started to fall in love with each other, and some marriages and established relationships started falling to bits. There was this universal energy of love, and all of a sudden it could hit you with somebody else's partner. Because there was an openness towards anything that God sends in one's direction, some people would then – Richard, Lyle and myself included – dive into these relationships, and would find themselves in a tangle with no clear way of handling the complications.

16

It was like an epidemic. Not everyone involved was mature or sensible or experienced enough to know what was happening. I really feel it was an inexperienced or immature way of handling the powerful love energy that was pouring through the community. It really rocked the community, but it finally brought Findhorn down to earth and into a far more whole and inclusive sense of how we had to grow up.

After a couple of hours' work I go down to the Community Center for supper. Several community members, particularly those with families, are collecting their evening meal to take home for dinner. I join those eating in the dining room. After a washing-up stint at the kitchen sink, I go back to the caravan to feed the cat and do a few chores. Luckily my son, Lewis, requires very little practical looking after. He often washes the dishes and cleans up the caravan, particularly when he needs another accessory for his electric guitar!

8:15.   There is a community meeting tonight, and everybody is gathered expectantly under the multicolored lights of the Universal Hall. Amid the subdued hum of conversation before the meeting starts, Vadan, Nandano and Lissen are knitting quietly. Jeff is sewing a patch on his jeans. Linda is sketching faces in her notebook. Some of the older folk are settling back in their seats.

The lights dim. We start with a few moments of silence, during which Mark and Isha's baby hiccups. As the lights brighten, people look around at the baby and laugh.

The meeting takes a while to get under way. There is a lot of information to be shared about the forthcoming Midsummer Festival, and after other community business has been dealt with, we get to the main purpose of the meeting: to review our vision or overall plan as a community in relation to the growth-strain we've experienced in becoming what Eileen's guidance has called a planetary village.

David: *I've been here for over two years now, and I've seen my perceptions of the community change and expand. I came in response to the story of the Findhorn garden, which was very inspiring to me. The vision of the community itself has expanded: the Findhorn garden has grown to become a garden of the new humanity.*

Now it feels like a new pattern is beginning to emerge, moving us into another phase of the community's growth. Many of us are feeling it beneath the unclarity and the polarizations being expressed in issues that we're dealing with as a whole community. It seems that whenever we express polarities or take sides against each other, it is telling us about something more than an inability to make up our minds. It's telling us that something new is emerging. Lots of things have come up recently that would seem to indicate this: polarization around the issue of the number of guests that we have here in relation to the lack of housing space for our families and children; polarization around the continued physical expansion of the community when we're already deeply in debt. I'd like for us all to look at these issues and then look beyond them to a new vision of Findhorn that may be seeking to emerge at this time.

Daniel: *I've been going through a discovery in myself that I think is similar to what the community's been experiencing. Up until a year ago, I would hardly admit that I had a lower self, or at least I'd ignore it completely. I lived in the illusion that I didn't have to deal with my shadow and that all I had to do was to let the Light in, to meditate. My last year's experience in the community has changed my opinions.*

Looking at the shadow side of life, I discovered all sorts of things in myself and in the community that I didn't particularly like, such as jealousy, greed, and arrogance, among other things.

It was a very difficult time for me to be in a community where people had such high ideals. I looked at myself, didn't like what I saw, and tried to be different. I tried to change myself by using affirmations and meditations. What I didn't realize was that, not having accepted myself, I was merely strengthening my idealized self-image. So I became more and more frustrated, until I realized that my idealized self-image was not necessarily my higher Self but rather a mask for my lower self, which was very much like a little boy who develops all sorts of defenses, misconceptions, and wrong conclusions to cover his need for acceptance.

As a community I think we also have an idealized self-image to deal with. It often appears under the mask that we are really creating something "new", that makes us believe we are pioneering new forms of government, for instance. It is this mask which uses words like "guidance" to prevent us hearing the authority of others. Unless we learn to accept the authority of others by opening ourselves to experience the healing pain of not always getting our own way, we are only demonstrating our illusions. The question of accepting each other's authority involves being totally honest and open to challenge, being committed to look for our own mistakes, and being willing to expose any negative intent. And that takes courage.

I would like to suggest that we start looking at our idealized self-image as a community, to describe it and see where we sell it to the outside world, to expose when and where we do not live up to this image, and to reaffirm the true vision it masks.

François: *I've come to see the community's evolution, over the years, as a process of unfoldment from one aspect of our identity to another. In David's words, "Each stage becomes the womb for the stage to come, and as the new stage emerges, it shatters the womb of its previous incarnation."*

Whenever old boundaries are transcended there is always a period of what seems like chaos and confusion until the new boundaries of identity are defined and in turn outgrown.

The dangers of this process come when an individual or group identifies with any one of the identity-aspects we grow through; because really we don't have to limit ourselves by choosing between identities. So we don't have to choose between being an ashram or a community, or being a school or becoming a village. In a way, one can see each of these identities as facets or sub-personalities of the whole which transcends and unites these various aspects.

Our vision, as I see it, is not a crystallized perspective of our future development. It is something that is always unfolding as a result of the feedback we receive. We're always getting feedback both from within the community and from the outside world, and there's always a grain of truth in even the wildest feedback, which has helped to balance us out in some way. In evolutionary terms we should be grateful for our degree of non-equilibrium, *because it is only through it that an open system can not only withstand the influx of other energies but actually synthesize them so that the whole system is raised into a higher order and complexity.*

When all have had their say, the meeting ends with a meditation.

We open our spirits to the eternal Presence of the Light. We open our minds to the thoughts and creative visions and dreams that are shared by our fellow community members. And we open our eyes to the Light streaming forth from each other. And we give thanks.

At this time of year it does not get dark at night. The sun dips below the northern horizon, skims beneath the earth's rim, and rises again a few hours later. There is just enough darkness to see the stars.

Back in the caravan, after the community meeting and a couple of beers, I check my son's room: he's not home yet. Before turning in I light a tall green candle and leave it for him.

Emptiness comes flooding in. Snatches of thoughts flare into concentration like moths into the flame. And the end of meditation is death . . . Everything becomes meditation . . . People are almost invisible, vanished inside, almost gone . . . we are not "human beings" – that is just a notation. We are all divine beings, and there is no word in the dictionary for us.

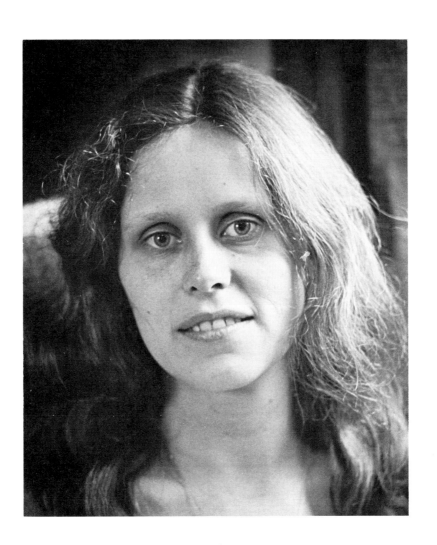

Peter and Eileen

P*eter:* People often ask me how to go about starting a community such as Findhorn. One way you don't do it is by advertising for others to come and join you. That's putting the cart before the horse, and it's not the way to attract people anyway.

The people are important and what they are is more important than what they know, but first you must have a vision. You need to have a vision of why you want to start a community and then sound that note and those who resonate to that note will be drawn to you.

Also in my experience, you must be sure you're going to start a center in the right place: it needs to be in a place of spiritual power to which you feel really drawn. It is as if there are nodules or acupuncture points or chakras in the Earth and it is at these places that centers of Light should be started. Different centers will start in various places for different purposes. Just as there are different acupuncture points or chakras in the body and each one has a particular function, so it is with centers.

However, the real question is not, "Am I starting a community on the right land or the right power point?" but rather, "Is it really God's will for me to start a community?" If I can be sure of that, then all these things will come.

If you are guided from within to form a center, then it's worth remembering that it's the foundation that takes the time in constructing a building, because it has to be solid. The groundwork has to be dug deep. It has to be strongly based on the God within, so that the whole structure can withstand the storms and stresses that undoubtedly will come later.

A community needs to be clear about its own identity with its vision. If people come and they don't identify with that vision, then it should be made clear that it's the wrong place for them. They should go to another group that is more in harmony with their vision of a new age center. So it is important that you keep a clear vision of what the role, function and purpose are for each particular center.

To start a community I believe you need strong leadership – with the vision to get it under way, and with the ability to make decisions. Then later on you can evolve into group consciousness. I know of no successful community that started as a group. Findhorn itself was started with strong leadership, and now it has moved more into group consciousness, group work.

It's also essential to stress that a strong initial vision isn't the same as a blueprint. Supposing we had been told right at the beginning what Findhorn was going to develop into? We wouldn't have believed it. So we were just given a little bit at a time, and that led us to the importance of living in the moment, in the "now", concentrating on one step at a time and finishing off to perfection one job at a time. You can only do that if you are willing to be led intuitively from one stage of growth to the next.

Another vital lesson in starting to work with any building or area is to clean it from top to bottom. That clears out all the darkness and puts in vibrations of love and light. There is an occult reason for this, in that the forces of darkness can always find a niche where there is dirt and disorder.

We also learned how essential it is to start a new venture in a consciousness of love and peace. If any of us were in disharmony or upset or feeling negative, we would stop working and find that inner center so that the right vibrations could be put into what we were doing. Those vibrations are what set up a magnetic force field which draws people to you.

It's much easier to start a spiritual venture now. Eileen and Dorothy and I underwent long and rigorous spiritual training before we even came to Findhorn. I think people no longer need such drastic or rigorous training, though training itself is important; training in self-discipline, faith, obedience to inner prompting and being able to hear that still small voice within, being able to act on intuition.

I will give just one example of the sort of training I had in order to learn obedience to the inner prompting. The earliest spiritual training of Eileen and myself was given by my former wife, Sheena. She was a great soul but ruthless in her training methods. At one time, Eileen, Sheena and I were having coffee after dinner in a London restaurant. Half way through my cup of coffee, I had an inner prompting to go and see a friend named Jack. I finished my coffee, and left, saying I had a prompting to go and see Jack.

I missed him, though. I could not understand it. I came back and said, "I don't know why, but I have just missed him. I had the prompting when I was half way through my coffee." Sheena turned on me, told me that she knew psychically that this man had a revolver with him and had gone to commit suicide. She said that I'd missed him because, instead of following my inner prompting, I had followed my lower nature and finished my coffee. In fact, he had not taken his life, but for my training Sheena felt I had to believe that he had.

Once you have learned a lesson like that, you do not forget it very easily. Some years later when again the three of us were in a cafe in northern

Scotland, and I was half way through my cup of tea, I had a prompting to go and see someone on the South Coast of England, about 650 miles away. I was out like a shot without stopping to explain. With only a shilling in my pocket, I was out on the road, and coming towards me was a Rover car which I stopped. As it turned out, the driver was going all the way to London. She was a spiritual person and we had a marvellous talk; she also had a lovely hamperful of chicken which I ate with great relish.

If I had finished my cup of tea, I would have missed that lift and would probably have had to wait for ages for another.

I got to the South Coast, completed what I went for, and then headed back for Scotland. I got a lift in a truck out of London.

Sitting in the front of the truck at a traffic light, I looked down on a sports car which had a vacant seat. I said goodbye to the truck driver and got a lift in the sports car all the way to Carlisle, at eighty or ninety miles per hour.

If I had delayed and had not followed that inner prompting, the light would have changed to green, the car would have been away and I would have missed it.

I got to Carlisle and wondered how I would get to Oban. There was a fish lorry coming down the main street. I stopped it and got a lift to Oban. The driver seemed very sleepy. He had been driving for sixteen hours, so I asked if he would let me drive. I drove all the way through the night, and when we arrived at Oban next morning at 7:30, he was so delighted that he bought me breakfast.

The whole journey had been accomplished in less than four days. I could not have done it as quickly in my own car, and in spite of starting off

The Caddys – 1950s

with only a shilling, everything had been provided through having the discipline to act upon my intuition.

In 1972, when the community was well-established, David Spangler told me that I had developed the qualities of leadership in order to establish Findhorn, and now the leadership needed to be balanced with more love and understanding. Findhorn did not belong to Eileen and myself only, it belonged to its members, and once we had taken them, shall we say, through rebellious adolescence to maturity, the time had come to hand over responsibility. My next step was to awaken within me that side which could draw out and inspire people rather than appear to them as an authority figure. That was a big challenge for me – it was difficult to relate to people in that way while being aware of the things that needed to be done. It has taken many years, and the process has not been an easy one.

Once I had handed on the torch of leadership, I found that the flow of energy and inspiration was no longer moving through me in the same way. This really sank in one day as a party of us were driving to Erraid, with François at the wheel. Normally I drive pretty fast, but sitting next to him as we wound along the shores of Loch Ness, I thought we were travelling at an alarming speed, taking quite unnecessary risks. Each time we went around a blind corner I was

1976

terrified, thinking, "Good Heavens, I wouldn't have done that," until it dawned on me that only when you are in the driver's seat do you know with confidence what to do, what risks you can take. And François was now in the driver's seat, not I.

Interlinked with the changes of leadership and government within the community have been profound changes within Eileen and myself and within our relationship. Eileen and I were brought together like two soul halves to raise a family and help establish this community. We complemented each other as male and female, light and love, mind and heart, action and being. Together we made a whole. Our relationship was much more simple then, and became very challenging once Eileen was called upon to develop the so-called masculine attributes of independence, will and purposeful action and I began developing the more so-called feminine aspects of love, feeling and sensitivity. It was not easy for either of us. We reached a point where we felt it would be better for us to separate for a time, in order to continue our individual growth and find that balance as individuals.

I suppose, like many men, I find it difficult to understand women. With my long training in positive thinking I have been taught to control my emotions and deliberately choose what to experience. It is very difficult for a man like me to understand a woman's emotions, and I need to develop this understanding. I do not find that easy because I have never really experienced pain and suffering for myself.

The other aspect of developing the feminine part of myself has been to learn to rely on my own inner knowing. For me, this was speeded up once Eileen was told to stop getting guidance for the community or myself. Until then, God made sure that there was always someone there like Eileen, Dorothy, David and others to check with so that I could be absolutely sure my intuition was right.

Since then, my own inner knowing has been developing. I don't hear voices; I don't see visions; I can meditate until I'm blue in the face and never get anything – and then at the most unexpected times, like when I'm in the bath, or early in the morning, guidance comes in the form of intuition. It's no good trying to stop me once that inner knowledge happens! A vital aspect of the New Age is that each one of us learns to turn to the Divinity within. With that come the lessons of obedience and action. There's not much good in having an inner prompting if you don't act upon it.

I think that we are living in the most exciting period of history, a time of great change and transformation. How quickly this transformation comes about depends on how all of us experience it in our lives; how much love and light we can embody; how well we form together in groups and families to live in love and harmony. Centers of Light are emerging throughout the world as catalysts and points of stability, and the network of Light is growing stronger as people move between these centers. Times of political, social and economic turmoil are ahead, and I see that in coming years the world will need centers of stability, of love and light, balance and synthesis. It is important that these centers be linked up and that we each find that synthesis within ourselves.

29

Eileen: In October, 1971, I was told in meditation that I was to stop receiving guidance for the community, that each had to go within to find his or her own inner direction. I shared this guidance, and I stopped there and then. After that I was told to stop receiving guidance for Peter as well. That was one of the most difficult things I've had to do, because it threatened my whole identity; I didn't know what else my role could be. I felt completely lost, and it was hard for Peter and the community, too. It was like taking a baby off the breast suddenly, without weaning it. Of course, people still came to me. And I tried to help them, but never with guidance. I would get my own inner direction about what to say, but I would never give guidance to anyone.

It took me a number of years to realize that it wasn't necessary for me always to have guidance, to be the oracle; that I had to go within to live and demonstrate what I had received through thirty thousand pages of guidance. Now I'm just living it. It's like my lifeblood, and I feel it flowing through me.

From time to time over the past few years, Peter has sought guidance or confirmation from others. I used to find this hard at times. I would ask in meditation if I could get guidance for Peter, and I would be told that if I did, I would be holding up Peter's growth and evolution. I felt that because of my not receiving guidance for him, Peter and I were drawing further and further apart, and yet I felt that if that was what God wanted me to do, it must be right and best for both of us.

Eventually, I think Peter and I had to separate, for the present anyway, so that we could become two individuals first and foremost instead of two halves of a whole. It has been a question for both of us of trying to find a balance within ourselves. I have felt something of the power of that inner synthesis and of bringing the diverse elements together within me. Gradually, I feel I'm becoming a whole person, a whole being.

It has been the most devastating and yet the most wonderfully transforming time I have ever lived through. When Peter suggested we should separate, we were in Edinburgh at our son Christopher's graduation, and I was very angry. My pride was really hurt. I felt that I was a complete failure as a wife and as a woman. My guidance dried up. I was no longer needed by my children since they were all grown up. Now Peter no longer needed me. The community did not need me as they were working things out themselves and didn't need a "parent" image to help them. I was full of self-pity. I didn't want to go back to the community. I felt like a sick animal, and I wanted to find a hole to hide myself in.

Then I started receiving very clear guidance again. God kept telling me the last things I wanted to hear: I was not to divorce Peter. I was to wait, to be patient. I was told to go back to the community. I was to release Peter completely. God made things very clear to me; and I found that those times of stillness, listening to God, were my lifelines, although I didn't always like what I heard.

A therapist who is a dear friend of mine came to Findhorn to spend some time with me and help me shortly after I came back. She did a healing meditation with me. She took me up a spiral pathway to the top of a mountain, to a temple. I laid Peter and all my anger, frustration, jealousy, pain and hurt pride on the altar in the temple and gave it all over to God. She then said I was to visualize an angel standing there, and the angel was handing me a pair of golden scissors. Of my

own choosing, using my own free will, I was to cut the psychic umbilical cord that had linked Peter and me through the years. I cut the cord and tied a knot in it and placed it in my solar plexus.

During the meditation I found myself standing before a silver disc. I went inside the disc and stood in the middle of it. It was completely empty, but the inside of the disc was all silver as well. As I stood there, I heard the words, "Now accept the Freedom of the Spirit, the Joy of the Spirit." The silver from the disc poured into every atom and cell of my being until there was nothing left of me but pure silver.

Two days later I realized I was no longer attached to Peter. I was free, and, what was more wonderful, I could send love and blessings to him. It was a glorious feeling, and I kept thanking God for it. All my anger, jealousy, pain and hurt pride had gone. I could love as I had never loved before; love with God's divine love, unconditional love.

When we have found the balance of the masculine and the feminine within us, I know that we will not need to demand anything of each other at all. My aim is to find that complete balance within myself, with the knowledge that Peter and I will come together again if it is God's will.

About a week later, God said to me: "Now I want you to lay the community on the altar and give it to me." I was told that this was my biggest child, that I had been able to give up all my children, and Peter, and now it was time I gave up the community. I cried and cried; then I laid the community on the altar and gave it to God; and as I did, I realized that now I had given everything to God and I had nothing to hold on to. My security was in God alone.

I have put God first in everything in my life now, and my heart is overflowing with love, praise and gratitude. And I thank God for these tremendous gifts of freedom and for everything that has happened.

As far as the community is concerned, it is God's community. The spiritual roots have gone deep, deep down – nothing is going to shake them. I was told in meditation the other day, "The leaves may change with the seasons, the branches may be broken off with the winds of change and the storms of confusion, but the trunk is absolutely solid and steady, and the roots are very firmly established so that *nothing* can uproot them. They are there for all time." That is because this community is rooted and grounded in God; otherwise it would have crumbled a long time ago.

Although Findhorn has attracted a lot of attention in the last few years, and Peter and I have been invited to give lectures and workshops all over the world, there is nothing glamorous about our work. In some ways, it's very easy to be in the public eye. My own personal experience is that whenever life has become too glamorous for me, it's as if God takes me by the ear and puts me into a very ordinary, mundane position. And that's when you get down to the nitty-gritty. How do you cope? Can you love what you're doing? Can you really love washing those nappies? Washing the dishes? Cleaning the floor when the children come in with their muddy boots? These mundane things take all glamor away and you realize that you are learning to do everything with love, and therefore you are doing everything for the glory of God. Learn to love what you are doing, no matter how ordinary or how mundane it is. Do it. That's what Findhorn is all about. It's as simple as that.

34

Michael W.: *In a community where one's work is so closely linked with other people's, if one is out of sorts it's soon going to affect everyone else. The state of my relationship with anyone is the clearest reflection of the state of my consciousness. There is no escape. Any attempt to escape is bound to intensify the situation.*

Relationship and Community
Findhorn: Garden or Jungle?   *by Myrtle Glines*

Over the past few years, my co-worker David Spangler and I have been contacted by several persons who have felt that Findhorn was losing its direction or was becoming imbalanced in some way. We have also heard from people who had gone to the community in response to something they had read or heard, only to discover that its reality was not what they had expected. Most of these reports indicated a disappointment that, in the minds of these people, Findhorn was not living up to the beautiful ideals which it proclaimed.

This concerns me, for I have a deep personal interest in Findhorn's well-being and a love for the people who are trying to make it a success. My work there put me in touch with every facet of the community life and gave me opportunity to experience firsthand the challenges in building and running a place like Findhorn. These were not only the normal human relationship problems brought about by the presence of many strong and different personalities or by the community's small living area and limited accommodations which caused everyone to live in constant, close contact. There were also problems arising from the subtle but highly stimulating and transformative spiritual and psychological forces at work there.

This experience gave me a perspective on Findhorn's strengths and weaknesses, as well as an appreciation of the immense amount of commitment and care it takes just to make it work at all. It is important to remember that Findhorn does work, although not always to everyone's expectations. The experiences of Findhorn are not unique to that center either; I have found similar mixtures of positive and negative elements in every group or enterprise I have ever encountered. And just as the truth of an individual does not lie in his extremes, so it is true of Findhorn. Its reality lies neither in the glamorous image of a heaven on earth, nor in a picture equally negative. Rather, Findhorn is on a path of transformation, and we need to understand that path more clearly, for it is all of ours as well.

The most intense criticisms of Findhorn have come, as one would expect, from the people most involved with the community. I remember one young man who had come from London to live at Findhorn. He discovered, as do most who join the community, that Findhorn is no refuge from the problems of society. To the extent that these problems are inner, created through our own personal imbalances, we bring them with us wherever we go; and at Findhorn our inner contradictions are brought to the surface with uncomfortable intensity. This young man kept alternating between staying in London and living at Findhorn. Finally, despairing of his ability to adapt to Findhorn, he told us that emotionally it was a worse jungle than London.

Why should a spiritual center, based on ideas of love, service and wholeness, create such problems? Why should Findhorn be a jungle as well as a garden? One answer comes from the process of growth itself; another from the nature of the community and the people living there.

As a counsellor, I have found that the meaning of growth is frequently misunderstood. Many people seem to see it as a process of addition: the acquiring of new skills, knowledge, and images of self. To me, growth is a more profound activity than just acquisition. It is a deepening into the wholeness of life, like the spreading of roots to nourish and support the visible structures of stem, leaves, and blossoms.

36 **Mary:** *We now use several personal growth techniques to assist us when we get stuck – co-counselling, psychosynthesis, rebirthing and different forms of meditation. Yet the techniques are not ends in themselves – they are a means of enabling people to look at and take responsibility for the whole of themselves, to transform elements within themselves that hold them in old patterns. All the techniques, in one way or another, acknowledge a higher vision of humanity and are working to bring it about.*

Kay: *Floyd and I have been married 36 years, and we went through a lot of pain for years before we came here, working on our emotional attachments. If we'd come to Findhorn any earlier we wouldn't have been able to give much to the community. We would have been struggling with, "Is this person going to satisfy my needs, and if not, well, I'll try this person or I'll try this group or I'll be celibate for six months and see if that takes care of it." We reached the point where we both decided to retire from our respective careers, and we came to Findhorn having discovered through a long process of trial and error that no matter what you try, no technique, group or person is going to make you whole. Integration has to come from within.*

The Game of Life, a
growth tool created at
Findhorn, asks how we're
applying our spiritual beliefs
to our lives. At every turn
a player gets to look at
exactly this –
and respond.
Angé

It is a greater openness to life and its dynamic qualities. Growth can be joyous and exhilarating, a fulfilment of all that is most human within us. However, if we are unwilling to release our desires about how we should grow, if we shrink from confronting the deeper truths of our nature, then growth can be a challenging, frightening, and even a negative experience.

Within us is a mixture of characteristics, some of which we are happy with and some of which we aren't. These characteristics are the seeds we have sown over the years – our karma, if you like – or the tendencies we have built through our own habits. When we open ourselves to the forces of growth it is like exposing a garden to the sun and rain. Whatever seeds are there will sprout and reveal their nature, whether we want them to or not. This means we may find ourselves confronting unpleasant and undesirable elements within our nature. Also, for plants to emerge the soil must be broken up and the seeds themselves must disintegrate to give birth to new forms. Creativity often involves prior destruction and growth involves a giving up or a "destructuring" of familiar patterns to make room for new ones to appear. This process can produce imbalance in our lives. During growth periods, therefore, we are more vulnerable than usual, and more likely to experience negativity in our relationships with life.

The young man from London called Findhorn a jungle. Yet, a jungle is a place where the growth forces are strong and life is abundant. This is the nature of Findhorn: it is a place where the forces generated by the pioneering dynamics of life in its deeper aspects are exceptionally strong and concentrated, a tropical zone of the spirit.

Although its climate does not suit everyone, a jungle cannot be blamed for being what it is. Unfortunately, however, people coming to the community are sometimes unprepared for the intensity and swiftness with which inner pressures of change begin to manifest. While at Findhorn I observed that there were those who came expecting a garden of Eden, a community of loving souls where the problems of life would somehow resolve themselves. They came with definite preconceptions about both the community and their own growth. It was painful to watch the crises these people went through as their dreams ran up against the reality not only of Findhorn but of their own natures as well. Many people were able to readjust their expectations, but there were still those who refused to change or to give of themselves except in the manner that they wanted. These were the ones who eventually left the community with bitterness at what they saw as Findhorn's failure to adapt to their needs and desires.

Certain characteristics of Findhorn stand out as being most important to the understanding of the pressures of growth there. Primarily, Findhorn is a spiritual center, based on guidance from higher levels and on esoteric teachings. It has a deliberate focus on transformation and on exploring the frontier of a new consciousness as part of a greater planetary unfoldment. A creative relationship with invisible forces is an accepted and intimate part of the community's consciousness. The members identify their task as finding the blend between divinity and humanity, between a person and the whole of the universe, and all community activities relate to that task in some manner. And because we don't really know just what the nature of that blend will be, Findhorn tries to allow room for experimentation. As a center for exploration of the new, there is a real sense of pioneering and,

Kay: *At Findhorn we choose to be together with the whole idea of becoming one to serve God, to serve something greater than ourselves as individuals, couples or groups. We're still struggling with that process of surrender. By surrender I don't mean compromise, and I don't mean giving up individuality. I mean yielding attachments and personal desires in order to give as a team.*

Leona: *I've heard a lot about the New Age being an Age of Woman. What I think that means is that it is an age of the rebirth of the feminine principle to blend with the masculine principle which has been dominating most societies for thousands of years. It's not a return to the matriarchy of old that is needed, but a blending of the Yin-Yang principles in every aspect of our culture.*

Alice: *If our foundations as a couple had been weak, then they'd have been shattered by the extra load of community life. But if the foundations are strong, then the community is a great place to build on them. Coming here we found our lives much fuller; we share our meals with many other people, there's lots of questioning and discussion, and so much diverse activity that we almost have to make appointments to see each other! But it hasn't shaken our roots at all. It's given us that much more to come home to and share with each other. And I think that our marriage has improved because now we're taking the love that we're generating as a couple and we're doing something with it, which makes it even stronger. In a sense, joining the community as a couple can be like deciding to have a baby. Having a baby can fulfil a good relationship, but it may even help to destroy one that's seeking a fulfilment it isn't prepared for.*

consequently, very few rules of conduct; one looks to guidance through attunement to higher levels rather than to a code of laws. This openness to inspiration creates the sense that one needs to live in the moment, to be flexible and open to sudden change.

Findhorn exploded in growth and activity in the early 1970's, growing from a small group to a community of over a hundred. With this rapid expansion other pressures came to bear, with more jobs to be done than people to do them, and a sense of urgency to serve the rapidly expanding community. This high activity level, as well as the sense of experimentation and the strong spiritual focus, were the result of powerful growth forces invoked into the community life, and they fostered transformation in the lives of the members. At the same time, paradoxically, this same intensity made it difficult to deal with the consequences of that growth.

As imbalance and negative states of thought and emotion can be temporary by-products of growth efforts, the appearance of these states at Findhorn was intensified. Also, the spiritual nature of the community caused difficulty in dealing with negativity because it clashed with the community's high ideals and its emphasis on positive thinking. To give vent to negative pressures was to risk being seen as a disruptive element in the community's life. This was particularly true with respect to the community's general understanding of the Laws of Manifestation, through which Findhorn could attract to itself what it needed to grow and survive. Positive thought and emotion were seen as the fuel that made these laws work, whereas negativity was a neutralizing force that could block manifestation and thus threaten the community. Consequently there was a tendency to ignore the personality level, with its inherent conflicts, and concentrate on higher, more esoteric levels.

For many within esoteric disciplines the personality is seen as a "lower self", a source of distortion and error, something not to be understood but rather to be overcome, gone beyond, or transmuted. Because these methods are often not well understood, the practical effect of this approach can simply be to ignore the personality, hoping that by concentrating on a spiritual vision it will just go away somehow. Of course, it doesn't go away; it remains, untended and unintegrated, to be a source of continuing problems of relationship and communication on all levels. This way of thinking, though not extreme at Findhorn, tended to prevent some people from seeking help in dealing creatively with personality problems.

Added to this pattern was the tendency to find esoteric or spiritual explanations for almost everything that happened. This attitude diverted attention from inner causes of the problem and turned it outward, dispersing the sense of personal responsibility. It also tended to increase the repression of negative emotion and to make people feel guilty when these emotions surfaced. At Findhorn we faced a problem where the very nature of the place stimulated the appearance of negative emotional states as part of a natural growth process, while it also tended to deny an acceptable outlet to these feelings because they conflicted with spiritual ideals.

Despite these problems, the tendency to be critical of negativity within the community was offset by a generally good community perspective, a high level of humor and a great deal of love and caring.

40

Michael W.: *The other day I was struck by the situation in the lunch room. There is no question that the presence of children adds something vital to the environment. At the same time, I noticed that there was a lot of tension and mess around the tables where the children were. We occasionally have people saying that we should find separate facilities for the children, which is obviously ridiculous. Yet I could see how someone coming in from a hard morning's work, feeling up to here with all the pressures of the community, at least wants to be able to eat in peace. From a child's perspective, however, as you walk into the Community Center you see a lot of personal worlds battling for privacy. And the kids join right in to break down the walls, because they want communication, they want to feel acknowledged. So they make a noise until they are acknowledged.*

The paradox is that as soon as children know that you're willing to give them all your attention they don't need to demand it incessantly. Now I think that a good percentage of the community is becoming more and more available to giving the children the attention they need, because they're aware of the paradox that the more one is open and ready to give one's whole self to each little situation, the less one need fear being drained. The more responsive one is, the less friction one creates.

Michael W.: *I think that children are a beautiful example of how you can have your spiritual path staring you right in the face and yet not recognize it. It's so easy to feel that the kids are an interference, holding you up or preventing you from getting on with what you should be doing, because they're demanding everything of you. But that's all there is to the spiritual life – learning to give everything; children are a constant reminder of that.*

Clare: *I remember Milenko once telling us something that expresses ideally my vision of parenthood. When Cathi was pregnant, Milenko was once meditating and he felt the soul of their unborn child communicating with him and saying: "I'm choosing you to be my parents because I know that I'm going to go through all kinds of experiences in my life that will put me in danger of forgetting my true Identity, and I'm choosing you to be my parents because I know that you will always remind me who I really am."*

42   Irmeli: *The night before Debbie's wedding she had a party for her women friends in the community. It was like a tribal gathering. There were about thirty of us, all sitting around in a circle. Debbie's mother and sister were there, too. I sat with my head in the lap of a pregnant friend and felt warm and relaxed. There was such a nourishing, feminine,* present *energy in that small room.*

People were sharing their experiences of love and marriage. I was struck by the power of the sharing and people's openness about things that aren't usually easy to talk about: their intimate feelings and fears and expectations about sexuality and marriage, and their disappointments as well.

Everybody shared about all kinds of relationships, from life-long partnerships to lovers that had been gone the next morning. When my turn came, I was a bit inhibited at first, but then I felt that what we were doing was offering our own special wedding gifts to Debbie. I wanted to be as honest and open for her as possible because I felt that she was very young and excited about getting married, and she was very willing to listen and learn from other women's experiences. It felt like giving her something that she was ready to receive. In that sense it was as though we were participating in an ancient ritual in a spontaneous reawakened form.

The whole evening was very revitalizing. It was like wiping the dust off the mirror of our relationships and seeing them, and seeing our images in them, more clearly. There was a sense of affirmation, not just for our present relationships, but for the past ones, too. The whole ritual was like a blessing of those past experiences and an integrating of them into our present. It was a harvesting and a blessing of all our shared experiences.

Experimentation and the high activity level in the community added the element of instability to the pressure of growth at Findhorn. Growth is a process of deepening, not just activity, in the direction of newness and change, and because it can create its own temporary experience of instability, it is good if growth can be nourished by a stable environment. The constant intense activity within the community, though not in itself a bad thing, did, however, further complicate the process, substituting a sense of motion and change for a slower, more gradual deepening.

All these factors detracted from the overall stability of the community and so also had their effect on family life. The demand of the community for the greater part of an individual's time and energy had a dispersing effect on families that came to live at Findhorn as well, bringing into conflict the allegiance of husband and wife to each other and to their children with their new allegiance to the community.

Families have never had an easy time of it at Findhorn, and some have been broken up. However, I observed that in every case where a family broke up in the community, the seeds of that separation were already there before the couple came to Findhorn. The community simply intensified and speeded up their confrontation with the realities of their relationship. Also, the glamor of growth, of moving into a New Age and leaving the past behind, tended to devalue that which was familiar and ordinary, such as day-to-day chores of home building and parenting. Instead it gave a lustre to that which was new and different and seemingly more significant. Thus, working in the community, building a New Age, grappling with metaphysical problems, seemed more exciting and more meaningful than the chores and duties of the householder. All of this, as well as individual internal growth pressures, put strain on relationships and family life.

Life at Findhorn was further intensified by there being few rules, placing a premium on self-discipline. But self-discipline is also a matter of training and can be difficult to develop in the vulnerability of an intense growth process. As a consequence, Findhorn can appear as an emotional jungle where people are left exposed to the heat of the sun and unprotected from the ravages of their own contradictions and those of the community. The fact remains, however, that Findhorn has been meeting its problems and continuing to grow. Findhorn does have its jungle aspect, but it is learning to deal with it in creative ways. Today the focus is still on expanding beyond personal concerns to contribute to the larger whole, but within that focus more flexibility has been created for the necessary personality work to be done.

People look to Findhorn seeking a garden rather than another jungle. Most people feel they already live in a jungle in modern society and long for inspiration and for a piece of heaven on earth. But, because Findhorn is a physical place, its concreteness can obscure its vision. People hear of it, and rather than see its reality within their own lives and environments, want to travel to Scotland.

We see and hear what we wish. We create our dream worlds and try to project them into reality. We desire a heaven on earth. We can have such a heaven if we are willing to create it in our own lives and where we are, which means confronting the challenges of growth. This is all they are doing at Findhorn. The problems that arise are human problems; the triumphs are born out of the spiritual potentials and realities within all human beings everywhere.

44   Babs: *Three of us went to visit Alan in the hospital the day he died. We knew he was in intensive care, but none of us knew he was dying until a doctor came and spoke to us in the waiting room. Then we had to wait a long time before a nurse came to get us. We talked about death, and our experiences and fear of it, and we had a quiet time together. As we were walking down the corridor towards Alan's room, I suddenly felt such a rush of joy that it was hard to contain it. I couldn't understand it because when I'd been a nurse before coming to Findhorn I'd been with many people who'd died, and my memories were not very pleasant. When we went into the room the nurse, to my surprise, left us behind the curtains by ourselves. Alan was lying there, totally unconscious, on a monitor. We stood still for a few moments, then we decided to attune, holding hands with Alan, around his bed. Again this rush of joy came, and when I opened my eyes I saw the monitor needle had stopped pulsing. He actually had died while we were meditating with him. Afterwards we drove home and I felt so inexplicably happy that I couldn't sleep that night.*

Three days later Alan was buried in the cemetery behind Cluny Hill. It was a glorious day. There were about thirty of us there, and we carried the coffin and lowered it into the grave ourselves. Then we meditated and sang together, and I almost felt like dancing. Afterwards, on the way home to Cluny we passed a newborn foal struggling onto its legs. I suddenly realized what a change of perspective I'd been through. I'd glimpsed that life and death are indivisible, and that death is a process of transformation and not of loss.

Wedding Celebration

Bart: *The energy at my daughter's birth held my attention so strongly that I couldn't talk. It was a constant meditation. When the head actually started to crown and I could see a little patch of hair, a wave of gratitude and joy and a feeling of specialness at being present at this birth just washed over me. The birth was happening to me too, and I was so grateful that I started crying what could have become uncontrollable tears, and I would have missed it all. I just let the feeling fill my whole body, and stayed aware of what was happening. When the head came out, I wondered what the difference is between life and death. It was strange to see this creature that was moving and kicking but was not breathing. It wasn't alive, yet it was. It was alive on some other plane of existence. It was mysterious and kind of grey, like a stone; it wasn't human-being-colored yet. When it came out it made a little crying noise as it took its first breath. Nobody said a word. We just listened. We were listening and watching, hearing her gentle breathing, and seeing the snow falling gently outside. That was when I began to love her, when she first breathed. I still couldn't talk. Then I picked her up, and she opened her eyes. Everything was so peaceful. She looked at me with this ancient look of wisdom, checking me out. Then there was a feeling of oneness . . . letting her know I was there . . . that this is a safe place to be . . . that she had come from one womb into a larger womb. I never felt love like that for anything or anybody. I watched her change color from grey to pink; I watched the life come into her.*

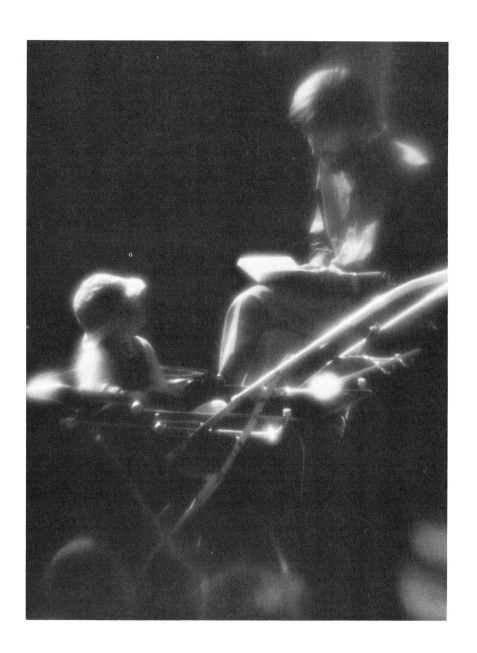

Cluny Hill

Findhorn Foundation
Cluny Hill College
Forres IV36 0RD,
SCOTLAND

Dear Family or Friends,

Here at last is an attempt to put into words the very deep and expansive experience of having lived here for three months.

I live in what used to be a grand old hotel — it's immense! There are almost a hundred bedrooms with very high ceilings, a ballroom, several lounges, enormous windows, turrets, chimney pots and much more. It is built against a hill and has several levels. One day my housecare job was to wash all the fire doors, which meant going through the entire maze from top to bottom.

Having always been around a lot of people, and having yearned for privacy, the first few weeks were tough because of the intensity of living closely with so many people. Of those here, ninety are guests, coming in each week for programs and workshops. Now I have a room of my own — a real blessing here, and place, people, and patterns are becoming more familiar.

Being an early person, my day starts at about six a.m., with a long walk in the woods before breakfast to greet the sunrise. Personal and linking meditations before leaving my room. Early rounds of sanctuary, lounge, kitchen — starting the new day. Despite its immensity, Cluny is my home while I live here.

After breakfast I watch for the mailman and hope he arrives before the bus leaves. Findhorn is about five miles from Forres and people flow back and forth between them. I work with Publications and so commute daily to the caravan park at Findhorn. I must dress myself for an ever-changing climate. Sunrise may be followed by snow, sunshine again, rain, a feeling of spring, cold sleet — all within our work day. Many rainbows, winds from the North Sea, gulls and crows together over the fields. The flocks of sheep we pass daily should be lambing soon...

Bennie

Saturday morning guest arrival at Cluny

56 **B**efore we purchased Cluny Hill we had months of negotiations. Then there was one final meeting when the company which owned the hotel suddenly told us, more or less, to put up or shut up within twenty-four hours. The rub in that particular situation was the timing. Many people in the community felt that getting Cluny Hill at that time was not on – it would stretch us too much. We had an all-day core group meeting, and it was split right down the middle. Half the people said, "Let's go ahead now," and the others said, "No, if we wait, it will come to us on exactly the terms we want." Essentially what happened in the meeting was decision-making by attunement. After our initial meditation and our split, we reattuned. We talked a little more, loosened up, had another meditation. Finally, despite our initial polarization, we recognized an energy flowing through us which said, "Now is the time." Everyone had that recognition.

Vance

Cluny is the main gateway into Findhorn, or Findhorn's main gateway into the world, whichever way you want to look at it. At times it can seem more like an airport or railway terminal than a community. On Saturday mornings, for instance, you see guests arriving, thronging the hallway. You see piles of luggage everywhere, expensive pigskin cases next to tattered carrier bags containing little more than a toothbrush and a damp pair of jeans. And all these guests carry with them as many different kinds of preconceptions about what this place is going to be like – you see them going through confrontations from the very start between what they experience and the images and projections they have brought with them from their readings of the visionary founding of the community. Yet week after week you see people touch through to the essence within themselves and literally be transformed.

Ralph

Until we bought Cluny, we'd been about two hundred people living in a caravan park without much room for the guests who were being drawn to the community in increasing numbers. It was always a bit like a jigsaw puzzle trying to find a place here or there where we could fit in a visitor for a while. Now, through our guest program, workshops and conferences, Cluny has enabled us to have a constantly revitalizing contact with the world.

Carol

Petra: I came to Findhorn from the Auroville community in India three years ago. In many ways it was a shock to come here, seeing with the eyes of Auroville and of India. Our life was much simpler there. Everything was used to the full. There was no waste. You cleaned your house with a broom, not a vacuum. If you broke something, you had to fix it, because there was no replacement. You had few clothes and you washed them in the evening so that the next morning they'd be dry and you could wear them again.

When asked at Findhorn to grate carrots in the kitchen I refused, because at Auroville we had to cook for about fifty people and I would have had to grate all morning by hand. I thought I just couldn't do the same thing for three times as many people. It never occurred to me that there'd be a machine to do it.

What made me stay was the people. I think what struck me most was their faces. Even now I don't know clearly why I stayed, but that's what drew me – the purity of people's eyes. And the openness. I felt more at home than I had at Auroville.

Findhorn's organization was also a shock for me. I hadn't been expecting such organization. If I had, I probably would never have come. But I was attracted right away to Cluny Hill. As one of several Dutch people living at Cluny, I feel very much at home in its hard-working, outgoing atmosphere.

Petra van der Berg

I began by working in the dining room. It was just before Findhorn's first conference. Working at Cluny during that first conference time, I felt like a fish in a very big sea. There was so much excitement and discussion and change and so much to organize and do. The dining room was a microcosm of it all. I had to get away after work to walk in the woods. Yet I loved it.

I worked there for six months, during which time I went through a separation with the man I had lived with for five years. In a community as close as this, everyone knows right away what's happening in your life. I would come to work and people would give me such support. And I changed a lot. After we separated, we both lived apart here for two years in this same building. So we had a chance to work everything out. But it wasn't easy in the beginning.

Life is intense when living with a family of sixty plus ninety house guests in one building. At first I found it hard to be always so

Stained glass in Cluny Sanctuary

I'm learning that all of the so-called good and bad qualities we see in each other are actually a reflection of something that's in ourselves. Look at me and see yourself. For me, this recognition has been the first step towards self-acceptance. It's an acceptance which needs to encompass both the shadow and the angel in us all.

Mary

involved in the strong energy field of the place. Now I feel I can recognize the undercurrents without being drawn into them. Sometimes the whole building buzzes with the energy of a particular guest group or workshop. On Thursday there was a "Game of Life" workshop in the ballroom, and you could feel its effect in the kitchen, the laundry and even the garden. We once had someone draw a picture of Cluny as he saw it. He drew a big face which had sound coming out of the ears, flashes coming out of the eyes and noises coming out of the mouth. That's how this building can seem to people. I can feel the weight of the dining room above me right now. I can feel what's going on in there. Every part of the building presents to me a different, almost tangible energy. Sometimes I think of it in terms of parts of a body: the dining room is the solar plexus, the kitchen is the heart, the Beech Tree Room, where the workshops meet, is, I think, the mind of the building, and the sanctuary, the soul. The ballroom, and sometimes the bar, can also serve as vital organs.

After half a year I moved to the kitchen to set up the bakery. I went to a nearby bakery first and baked there for a couple of weeks. That's how I started to get in touch with the local community. In Auroville, I had worked with the local people, and I missed that here. Afterwards, when I worked as a buyer for the kitchen, my contact with the local people increased, and it meant a lot to me. I feel that with many of them, there is a strong spiritual connection – only they may not talk about it in spiritual terms.

A year-and-a-half ago, I was asked to join the guest department. At first it was frightening because I didn't know what was expected of me as a guest group focalizer. I found it hard until I discovered that the only thing that was really required of me was to be myself. Now it is wonderful; each guest group is so different and each has its own quality and purpose in coming together. I'm always surprised by the different ways groups work out. I feel that we are not only creating an opportunity for people to experience the community, but also a place to facilitate their coming together and opening up to themselves and to each other and experiencing their unity. It's very simple; that's what the strength of the community is. And that's what we're all doing – working through our changes, learning to use the positive aspect of apparently negative situations, being there for each other, discovering that each of us makes a difference in the world.

Living at Cluny Hill is a twenty-four-hour-a-day job. With so many people living under one roof something unexpected can happen at any moment. People knock on my door at night and want to talk. There's a lot of concentrated energy in the building. Everybody's processes get speeded up. We need to be there for each other. That's why we're a community. It's good. It's very satisfying. And yet I notice that there are few people who stay more than a year at Cluny. There are only four people who've been here over three years. So we'd like to make it a little less of a transitory and crowded experience. It's fine as it is in many ways, yet I see ways for improvement: to have quieter areas, to create more space, more single rooms for people so we can find a sanctuary in our rooms to digest all the stimuli we've received and be by ourselves after having given out all day. Because that's what it means to live here: to give out all the time.

60   *When we first bought Cluny Hill in November '75, we found we had on our hands a pretty gloomy and neglected white elephant of a building. It took a tremendous amount of work to make it habitable. A work crew of twenty or thirty of us would come over from Findhorn each morning. We'd attune outside in a big circle before the day began. There was snow on the ground and it was an unbelievably cold winter. It was even colder inside. There was no heating and no running water. The corridors were all covered with polyethylene sheeting, dust and plaster. The kitchen had to be steam-cleaned half-a-dozen times and totally dismantled. People were hammering and plastering and painting and working with blow torches to turn the old billiard room into a sanctuary. It was bitterly cold, and the work was exhausting, yet there was a tremendous dynamism and group unity. In April we had our first conference, on Transpersonal Psychology, followed shortly thereafter by our first guests. Those few months were a remarkable exercise in transmutation. We took this old, encrusted building, and transformed it vibrationally as well as physically.*

        Hugh

In contrast to a striking contemporariness I sense in people here, which has nothing to do with age (ranging at the moment from infant to octogenarian), is the building with its solid elegance of a century ago. And so you see backpacks resting against finely carved woodwork, sneakers making ancient sacred movements on the parquet of the ballroom, western Buddhists sitting zazen in the billiard-room-turned-sanctuary, with meditators from a dozen different cultures practicing at least as many spiritual disciplines.

Marjorie, *a guest*

Cluny has touched my heart, my
intellect, my deepest longings for
communion and community. I think
this is the way we will live in days to
come, for those of us who have the
courage to believe it possible and work
towards it . . .

63

I had expected flower children and
instead find scholars, mystics,
healers, artists, people committed to
their own and to the planet's
unfoldment. The morning workshops
take me to the edge of my imagination,
pique my intellect, make me feel wild
with the excitement of discovery and
sharing. My eagerness to know more,
to have points clarified, to stretch
beyond current boundaries, to
consider new possibilities are all met;
my questions are carefully responded
to and my curiosity honored. Rarely
have I encountered so little arrogance,
competitiveness, or dogma; there is a
tacit recognition that we are all on the
same path, asking similar questions of
each other and of life.
                    Marjorie

I think I had some expectations that this could be the "ideal" place — which I haven't found it to be. However, I've learned that the answers aren't in a change of environment — they are in a change of consciousness

Betsy

I'm focalizing the dining room. It's wonderful. You might think that wiping down surfaces, brushing chairs, and setting tables three times a day would be a mindless, boring sort of task. I don't know why, but it's exacting, exhilarating and amazing instead. I do know why, actually. It's because there's very little glamor to distract you from how you are resolving each moment. We aren't learning any skills. We are not professional healers. It's me and the dirty tea cups and messy snack area, and what am I going to do about it? How do you turn a pantry into a sanctuary? How does a dining room become a nourishing, healing environment? It's obviously as mindless and boring as counting pine-cones in the forest . . . and it's a challenge to answer the questions; but it has a great deal to do with purity and love and service.

Joy

Damien

It's a real challenge to support family life here. It's tough to maintain a sense of home. Community living is a full-time job, and it's undoubtedly easier for single people.

But family life is an incredible teacher, and people who have had that experience are really valuable in the community. My thirteen-year-old son, Damien, is a total bonus. Just having him is a gift. He pushes me and stretches me; he's my guide and my anchor. I could spend my life getting upset at Damien, working it out myself, reminding myself that he is not me. I think Damien learns very little from what I say to him. He just comes in and says, "I've heard you. Look at your room. It's a mess. You sit here telling people to clean up their acts and their relationships and your floor's a mess." It's perfect, absolutely perfect. I don't like it.

Joy

What do you do when you're feeling depressed or uptight, and you're living in a place where love and light are the accepted norms? It's both easier and harder to experience your own negativity here. It's easier because the environment is supportive, because people give you space; they accept you whatever you are feeling or expressing. It's harder because there are so few places to hide – since we all live together in a relatively small area, everyone can see what's happening in your life, and you're always getting feedback.

Ange

70   **T**here are sixty residents here and, like most of those I've spoken with around Findhorn, they struggle to find a balance between personal and group need, activity and receptivity, self-nurturing and nurturing of the whole . . . Although I see weaknesses, problems, areas that sooner or later will need to be confronted, I trust the goodwill that underscores a powerful commitment to the light and love of this community. If there is a constant here, it is that everything about Findhorn (and Cluny, of course, as one of its manifestations) seems continually in flux, movement, subject to change.

It will be difficult to leave because I'm thriving here. In asking of me the best that I can be – fully conscious, participating, loving – this experience has led me to glimpse my part of the whole. That, happily, is portable, and I intend to take it home with me to cherish, nurture and use with abandon.

Marjorie

Celebrations at Cluny

It strikes me that both Findhorn, as a caravan park, and Cluny, as a former hotel, are images of transience. And that reminds me of a favorite quote of Sir George Trevelyan's: "Our greatest truths are but half-truths. Think not to settle down forever in any truth; use it as a tent in which to pass a summer night, but build no house of it, or it will become your tomb. When you first become aware of its insufficiency, and see some counter-truth looming up in the distance, then weep not but rejoice: it is the Lord's voice saying, 'Take up your bed and walk.'"

Dennis

Politics and Synergy

Nick: *Working in groups as we do at Findhorn, seeking group attunement in decision-making has been an instructive process for me. I have very ambivalent feelings about groups. I would say that a number of people who are drawn to the community are not naturally gregarious, and certainly I would include myself as a person who's not particularly comfortable in working with groups. I often find the process tedious, irritating, mediocre, and frustrating. Yet I recognize that potentially a group may be more creative than each individual working on his or her own. I believe in the concept of synergy, and that the evolution of consciousness is reflected in the increasing complexity of life forms. Thus I feel that a number of individuals working together can create an entity which potentially can embody a greater aspect of divinity than any one person alone.*

Ralph: In a community where one of the principal objectives is for all members to learn to direct their lives by their intuitive sense, how *does* order emerge from what might seem to be a recipe for chaos? What is the nature of spiritual government and organization in which the essence of each individual is respected while the central guiding vision is maintained and the good of the whole fostered? As Findhorn has grown from a single caravan with three adults and three children to a community/village, the development of appropriate governmental structures has been and remains a key challenge.

Rue: *Spiritual government is not the imposition of an outside force, but a growing awareness and active demonstration of inner qualities, which are actually the reflection of universal laws. The function of government, then, is not to make and enforce laws as if*

life were reluctant to obey, but to perceive that the real laws, the real power, are in the very nature of life creating itself. Our role is to recognize the inherent harmony of that creation and to give it clear human channels to move through. I'm coming to understand that what we call "government" grows out of a set of beliefs about human identity. The government of a people can only be a reflection of that people's idea of who we humans are, what our purpose is and how we should behave towards each other. At Findhorn, we are saying that our identity is divinity, our purpose is service, and our power is co-creation through love.

Matters were simpler in the sixties when Eileen received guidance and Peter put it into action. While the foundations were being laid, the community was governed and directed through one man's powerfully focused implementation of a spiritual impulse. All who lived at Findhorn at that time accepted the need for a strong man at the helm whose energy and practicality could implement the spiritual vision. Peter's faith and dedication were such that there was no question of deviation from the purity and power of the guidance. All who experienced this form of leadership recognized that it bore the stamp of a divine, not personal, will. His – and the community's – obedience to Eileen's vision was total.

In 1971, however, Eileen was told by her inner voice to stop sharing her guidance with the community. The purpose of Findhorn was not to develop good-willed, obedient servants. Rather, it was to be a place where people could come to know their *own* Godhood, each learning to act from his or her own initiating center.

Crispin: *I don't subscribe to the idea that any one person or group holds the vision for the community.*

The vision is available to anyone who can attune to it and be responsible for it. And that can be people throughout the community, not necessarily in positions of authority . . . especially when someone with authority leaves or steps down; that gives you the space to recognize the authority in yourself.

74

Vance: *At all levels of decision-making, there is a willingness to work less from personal desire here. If a pattern of ego dominance comes up in a situation, it is easily recognizable because so many people are aware of it and willing to deal with it. The object is to allow a decision to reveal itself so that the appropriate action becomes apparent to everybody.*

As Findhorn expanded rapidly in the early seventies, the sources of guidance broadened as well. David Spangler arrived at the beginning of this phase with his spiritual colleague, Myrtle Glines, and filled many roles in the three years that he was here: crown prince, high priest, court jester and resident sage. His awareness, along with Myrtle's, provided the community with a continuing source of wisdom, insight and direction. In 1973, however, David, Myrtle and Dorothy Maclean, along with some twenty other community members who held key positions of responsibility, moved to the U.S. to found the Lorian Association. A year-and-a-half later, R. Ogilvie Crombie, another of the community's guiding elders, died.

It was a time of new beginnings for Findhorn. The community's immediate access to transcendent sources of guidance and direction was no longer available. What emerged instead was a commitment to group consciousness and attunement, with the need for each individual to seek his or her own transcendent source, sense of direction and motivation. Findhorn continued to be a spiritual community guided by the God within. Only now that voice was no longer to speak with the accent of one or two individuals whose alignment with the Divine was unquestioned. It sought expression through a broader source, encouraging the whole community to turn within for guidance.

Helen: *I feel that guidance comes through a group like pieces of a puzzle being added. When we have a group meditation, different people bring different aspects. Intuition is influenced by one's background, environment, training and education. What I see happening in all the groups in the community is people trying to work together from a space of clarity.*

Leona: *At its highest, a group seeking to make a decision comes to a point of fusion. When an issue is brought up it's important to examine it fully, and then move into meditation holding that question in mind. Fusion comes through the development of trust within the group. If anyone goes into the meditation mistrusting any one person or the situation, it doesn't work.*

Meanwhile, the community had grown considerably. By 1973, Peter had already realized that the community was becoming too large for him to run alone. There were now many different work areas or departments. Each one had its own responsibilities and decisions to make, and the role of "focalizer" had evolved to guide the work of each department and co-ordinate decisions. These focalizers began to meet each week to discuss community affairs and their departments' needs.

Sarah: *I always felt that being a leader meant that you were responsible for keeping an organization running. At Findhorn a focalizer is not this kind of*

ELIXIR
27th March 1974

Why waste time and energy discussing and arguing about a problem and how to handle it?
Why not be still and in the silence go within and let Me reveal the truth to you. Never
try to work out a solution with the mind, let the mind be your servant, never the master
Use the mind to work through but not with it

This is something the core-group needs to learn to do so each solution and decision
comes through the intuition and inspiration. This will come in time when all
of you can see and accept that I AM running this Centre of Light, that I AM there
to guide and direct each one of you that I AM within each one of you and when
you are all attuned to Me you will each reach the same solution, for I AM the
Universal Mind. No problem is too small to bring to Me. See the core-group
functioning from that Universal Mind and then everything will run
smoothly and there will be perfect harmony and Oneness.
Simply know it will come and never despair.

Excerpt from Eileen's Guidance

leader. *For me, focalizing the maintenance department
is like being a funnel through which one pours water
into a bottle. A funnel directs the water into the bottle,
but the energy for the action is not in the funnel, it is in
the water. It's a service you are providing, a particular
input into a circle of people.*

Stephen: *Leadership at Findhorn is based on a
hierarchical pattern not of power, but of responsibility.
If my responsibility, as focalizer of the publications
department, is to ensure that deadlines are met, the
way that's carried out is not to insist that someone meet
a deadline but to share, in the most open and clear way
possible, the reasons for it to happen. Being a focalizer,
holding a broader awareness of the way a whole system
operates, I try to share that awareness and allow each
person to contribute his or her part.*

As Findhorn grew and gained in fame, Peter
and Eileen began going out from the community
on tours which kept them away for extended
periods. The question of governance in their
absence was resolved by the creation of a "core
group" consisting of a small number of trusted
individuals whose purpose was to attune to the
vision and direction for the community and
reflect that vision in decisions of policy. In time
this group was to be faced with making decisions
of critical import in the absence of the
community's founders. For example, while Peter
and Eileen were away in 1975, the core group
made the decision to purchase Cluny Hill Hotel,
committing the community to a £60,000
investment and a marked expansion of its
education program.

76   Nick: *Over the past few years most of the groups I've worked with have been coming to terms with the question of guidance and what has been called the "democratization of guidance" within the community. That was one of the foremost issues I had to deal with when I was in the personnel group. Community members had been told to get their own guidance, but most people were rather sensitive if their guidance was ever questioned. I think it's like any new thing that you're not feeling totally sure about. People would come in and tell you that their guidance said that they were supposed to move from this department to that department next week, and I would say that's fine, but have you talked about it with the others involved. If they had talked about it, and it didn't feel to others to be in right timing for them to change jobs, people would still want to follow their guidance unquestioningly as they felt Peter and Eileen had done. I think a lot of our problems with guidance come from lack of discrimination and particularly from a misunderstanding of Peter's pattern, because Peter had told us so often that the test of a prompting was to follow it instantly. We expected that all we had to do was to follow our promptings at a moment's notice and, metaphorically, dash outside where there would be a car, with chicken sandwiches, on its way to wherever we needed to go.*

It's taken us up to now to accept the fact that guidance can come from many places including our own subconscious, or collective thought-forms in the community. And I feel that only now are we really prepared to start examining the sources of our guidance with some discrimination.

Vance: *As I spend much of my time these days in group meetings and discussions, I'm glad that I have spent a lot of time with nature. I am used to rhythmic, slow, organic growth where you don't see the results in a single season but over an extended period of time. That can be very much the way of meetings here, where decisions are reached through the process of attunement and consensus rather than majority rule.*

Craig: *When I was focalizing the core group, sometimes I would feel quite clearly what should happen and I would say it; other times I kept quiet because I didn't have any clear input. I was always trying to let the group experience itself and find what was coming out of itself. It's an educational process. Everybody in the group needs to be patient with the other people as they catch up or become aware of what's happening. Sometimes you're in front, and sometimes you're behind.*

Michael L.: *What gives me hope about Findhorn groups is that they are open to change. People come and go, so groups tend not to stagnate. Sometimes they even change so quickly that there's a problem of continuity and cohesion.*

Another thing I like is that when we as a group get stuck, we usually realize that we are stuck and take positive action, such as getting on with some other business, or meditating, or letting the problem rest and coming back to it later. Basically, we accept that many of the polarizations or difficulties that come up in a group can't be solved at the level of the mind and need to be transcended in meditation. Finally, if there's a minority who don't agree on an issue, the majority usually doesn't just steamroller over them and go ahead. In most groups my experience at Findhorn has been that where any major decision is being made, if two or three people haven't felt comfortable about something, then we've persisted until all present have been able to reach a point where they can support the decision even though they don't necessarily agree with

it. It's important that we take care, on the whole, to have group consensus, even though it may take a long time to reach it.

Findhorn continued with a hierarchical pattern of organization but, by 1975, the community was clearly beginning to take on its own governance and decision making. Since then, the emphasis has been on decentralization, so that people with direct responsibility for an area make the decisions and thereby take a more conscious part in shaping their lives. With the further sharing of responsibility, the question has arisen as to the interrelationship of the core group to the greater membership of the community. Recently a village council has been formed, which has representatives from all areas of the community. Its function is to examine fundamental questions of the vision and development of Findhorn and reflect to core group the community's feelings on any given subject. This structure provides the necessary vehicle to ensure creative dialogue between the policy-making bodies and the rest of the community. In addition, monthly community meetings draw the entire family together to share thoughts and feelings on current issues as well as to affirm our oneness.

François: *Everyone is recognized as having the ability to tune into the Universal Mind and offer his or her perspective and contribution to the government of the whole. This co-creative interaction leads to a government through synergy where individuals, knowing their own authority and power, are not threatened by each other but are working together to create a whole greater than the sum of its parts.*

As the consciousness of the community unfolds, so does its organization; no structure represents permanence, for Spirit is motion.

Towards a

Planetary Village

By 1970, Findhorn was moving from a group to a community. This involved a deep process of reorganization on several levels: visionary, governmental and economic. It took several years for the structural pattern to emerge.

At the time of the acquisition of Cluny Hill, the community was already bursting at the seams. Since then the communal identity has atomized itself into a collection of individual centers: the Caravan Park, Cluny, Drumduan, the houses in Findhorn Village, Marcassie, Cullerne, Newbold, Erraid and Iona.

We are again in transition – spiritually, politically and economically. One cannot point the finger to this or that event and say this is "where it began", since change and growth are always multi-directional, though they express the unfoldment of a single purpose. In 1969, Eileen had already received the following guidance:

"My Beloved, I want you to see this center of Light as an ever-growing cell of Light. It has started as a family group, is now a community, will grow into a village, then into a town and finally into a vast city of Light. It will progress in stages and expand very rapidly. Expand with the expansion."

François

We've worked through lots of images of ourselves as community. We've seen ourselves as an ark, a beacon of Light, a spearhead, a greenhouse, a spaceship, a kind of cosmic transformer, a garden, a university, a kindergarten, a mystery school, a planetary village, a training center, even perhaps a place to come and learn the piano. This latest one, the planetary village concept, is a mindblower because it's hard to relate the two words – one is futuristic and one is prehistoric. For me, at least, it's important to remember that we're not just returning to what Bill Thompson has called a windmills-and-granola agrarian fantasy.

Joy

There is a term in gestalt psychology which refers to the fact that when we perceive something we always see it as a figure against a ground, in a figure-ground relationship. Now the figure-ground relationship in the rise of the modern world was the city and the nation-state, so it was Manchester, Great Britain, or Manchester, British Empire. In moving away from international post-industrial civilization to the planetary culture, that whole figure-ground relationship is changing. Now it's more the small planetary village, like Findhorn, which moves under a different scale than the city and reverses the trend of urbanization. And that is seen against the ground of the planet, so it isn't Findhorn, Scotland or Findhorn, Great Britain, but Findhorn, Planet. In the same way it isn't Auroville, India, it's Auroville, Planet, and it's Lindisfarne, Planet.

William Irwin Thompson
*Planetary Culture and the
New Image of Humanity*

Opening blessing for the well

Rue: Two years ago the performing arts group was doing shows every Saturday night in the Lollipop Theater. One evening, when I was walking down from Pineridge on my way to the show, it occurred to me that I was in a town, in my home town, and I was going to the theater. My friends were putting on the show and I was in the audience. Shortly after that there was a community meeting in the Universal Hall, and it struck me that we were like citizens of a town coming to meet in our town hall. The unique thing about it was that all of us were both living in and running the town, and we'd built the hall ourselves. It seemed amazing and inspiring to me to be a citizen of this little town of Findhorn, living in it and creating it and being part of the running and organizing of it all at the same time.

Rue and Clarul Hass

Then I started thinking of all the different things you find in a town. You find churches and schools and government and business. So I looked around to see what sorts of things I could find like that at Findhorn. At first I thought of the Sanctuary as the church, but then I realized that while in one way that may be true, the spiritual aspect permeates everything we do. And so in a way the whole town is a church: it doesn't *have* a church, it *is* a church. And then I started thinking about the schools, and I realized that the whole place is a school, a mystery school, a University of Light, a universe-city. Everything we do we see as education.

We've grown through seeing ourselves as a university as well as a family and a community, but in doing so we've risked neglecting other important aspects of life, because it's much easier to sit around giving workshops about things than it is to actually do them. We want to be more than another workshop center. I believe that the process of exploring the new age university or college model has challenged us to become clearer in our thinking. I know that has been true for me. But it can become self-perpetuating – you can end up doing nothing but talk. Once you get something clear, the next step is to apply it in your life.

In towns like the ones we might have grown up in, issues tended to be things that someone else took care of while we looked after our own personal life. Living in this kind of situation, however, in this place of synthesis, we're really forced – or inspired – to at least look at everything we do in terms of a larger whole. Although this kind of participation by the people is the ideal of

Earth Ball Game

most cultures, it is rarely met. Most people experience a sense of political powerlessness and isolation.

I see some similarity between the changes we've been through at Findhorn and the grass roots political movements I was involved in during the sixties. Many people then were waking up to the realization that they themselves had power, they weren't just victims of other people's power. And they were beginning, for the first time, to take responsibility for the running of the university where they were students, or the business where they were workers, or the country of which they were citizens. Initially there was a lot of self-righteous anger, much of it destructive. In many ways it was a very shaky time. Looking back on it now, I can see how positive the whole process was. Sometimes what is presently happening at Findhorn seems very similar. When I see confusion and polarization, I wonder if it is not people once more beginning to take responsibility in unaccustomed ways and doing it initially from a somewhat emotional position. The tension has generated new forms, like the village council. There are also plans to enter more fully into custodianship of the land that's not a caravan park and to develop it as an ecological village.

In my own life I had to go through a period of experiencing the power within me before I could really accept power myself, and not feel obliged to express it all the time with anger or manipulation in my relationships with other people. And I think that is the next step for many people at Findhorn. Once people have claimed their

power and announced it and charged around using it, then the next step will be to give it up to God. And I think that's going to mean accepting that everyone has power, and trusting people with different functions so that everyone willingly chooses to play the role most suited to them while at the same time giving different and even apparently more powerful roles to other people. Whenever I've ended up in leadership positions, I have usually felt that I didn't know enough to do what I was doing. It took me awhile to realize that most people didn't know enough to do what they were doing, although not many would admit it. I think the same thing holds true for humanity as a whole. If we could just admit to each other that we don't always know what's going on without feeling embarrassed by our vulnerability, then I feel we'd be more ready to take the next step. That is, we'd be willing to trust that the power which moves all of life would move each of us in the right direction.

We're all going through growing pains at the moment, individually and as a community. We've made some big steps recently in terms of our physical expansion and in the way we see ourselves. We talk of being a planetary village and becoming a city of Light. In a way these are glamorous and distracting phrases. What's happening, I feel, is that we're going through a transition from learning to relate more clearly to each other as individuals, then as groups of individuals, and finally as groups relating to other groups. And we're starting to live lives inspired by spiritual principles rather than the materialistic or individualistic patterns that we are unlearning.

I remember Donald Keys talking here last year about planetary consciousness, and he said it was not so much an awareness of working within an international framework, but much more a matter of individuals around the world being able to embrace a consciousness of the whole planet in making everyday decisions in their own lives.
Michael S.

If there's one leap our consciousness has to make – and it's a quantum leap – it's how to be able to function, embody, look at and deal with multiple views of reality simultaneously and to be comfortable with that and not insist that reality only follow one particular course.

David Spangler

I always felt, especially when I first came here, that I was stepping into a time and space warp. Sometimes I would walk around feeling like I was somewhere in California. At other times, especially in the village or in winter, I would feel isolated on the tip of Scotland, but the caravan park is so anonymous it could be anywhere and all the caravans could be gone tomorrow. Then I would look around the different parts of the community and I would be amazed at all the different realities of architecture and forms: the old Scottish houses, the Hall, and above all the caravans; sometimes they seem like the most ridiculous sort of form you could imagine. That's what always strikes people when they walk in. I love seeing people's expressions when they walk in to the caravan park and say, "Well, where's the community?"

Patrick

The very incongruousness of our original caravan park setting points to the primacy of consciousness in the process of transformation. I've seen so many communities in the States that started by throwing up a lot of geodesic domes and structures and then collapsed because they had no integrated vision.

Richard

Herb Garden outside Community Center

Constantly coming in touch with two or three hundred other people is probably the greatest challenge I've ever had in my life. It's not like walking down the streets of Boston where people are surprised if you look at them. People here expect you to be aware enough of your own feelings, your own beingness, so that you can be open and share with other people, and not hide those parts of you that aren't feeling good, that are boring, that are difficult.

Stephen

The community has grown so big. I never quite understood the expansion. Sometimes it seems to me that it has just grown bigger and not grown better.

Now my life is saying "simplicity" to me. Boil down and find the real truths and live them. Tidy up your whole life. Make sure you are tying all the ends up before you go on to the next step. Don't take the steps too fast, until you've cleaned up and made sure you've finished the one before.

Lynn

Findhorn Village

When I learned a lesson in the community, it seemed as though it wasn't completed until I experienced it outside the community in the "real" world. As I talk to my sister-in-law, Marion, and more and more of the folks who live around here, I see that there isn't any great difference betwen "them" and "us". We have tools in the community that other folks don't have because we've had a long focused look at the New Age. But these people have the same knowing, especially here in Scotland where there's a lot of truth that's innate in the people because of the simplicity of their lifestyle, and because the area has been untouched by certain of the ills of civilization. I'd like to graft onto the local culture. I don't want to just spread a new culture over the whole area.

I think, basically, that the community is first planetary. It is so planetary that it's been ignoring its home base, which is Scotland. Sometimes it hurts me, because I'm married to a Scotsman. When I see lots of people who don't appreciate this place, it's not because the community is insincere, but because it's just so focused on something so much bigger than all of us that it doesn't see what is outside its own window.

Lynn

Vegetable garden

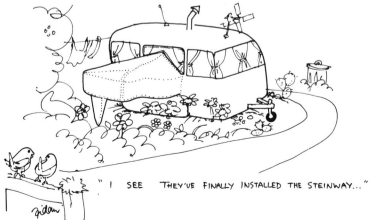

" I SEE THEY'VE FINALLY INSTALLED THE STEINWAY..."

Drumduan House

Cullerne House

At Marcassie, we were one of the first examples of the community's expansion into a village, and so we've had a new kind of relationship with the rest of the community. We were part of the whole, yet financially independent and going ahead as we felt guided in the development of this place. For the first two years we were constantly having meetings with the core group and other groups in the community and continually defining and redefining our relationship with them. This was one of the challenges. Since then, Drumduan, Cullerne, Erraid and Newbold have come into the community. We've noticed many similarities in what we're all going through, especially in continually being questioned and having to define oneself in the process of starting something new, which is difficult.
Christopher

Marcassie Farm

Helen Ruth, who paints mandalas, was working in the garden here last year. One day it dawned on her that she was working in a living mandala! That's how we see this garden. Phoebe

96   **W**hen the community continues to expand, and everybody feels stretched, it makes me release my vision of where we are going, and it brings me back to God. Things get bigger than I can handle, and part of me goes, "Gulp." I always feel we need to get things together, now, **before** we take new steps, but it never happens that way. I am never sure we're going to make it . . . are we going to blow it? Humanity has so often blown it. I wonder, "Do I fit in here anymore?" I like being in control, knowing where things are going, how it all fits together. When I'm doing so much and I feel so stretched, I get to the point where I feel I can't do it, I can't contain it by myself. Lately, when I get to that point, I say to myself, "I give up. God, you do it." And miraculously, God does. That's what keeps happening when I let go – everything falls into place, happens of itself. Times of strong feelings and fears allow us to let God more into our lives.

Mary

Findhorn Sanctuary

Station House and Sauna

SAUNA is HOT

Caravan interior

When we were asked to design possible models for the future development of the caravan park, we were puzzled about how to start. Then, the week that we decided to work on the project, two friends — both architectural graduates — arrived from Findhorn. We all sat down and meditated with a blank piece of paper. Our whole plan evolved from that meditation.

Greta

One of the problems with contemporary society is that it is based on a segregation of function. For example, in the village we come from in England everyone works outside the area, so the place is like a ghost-village in the daytime. At Findhorn we felt we should avoid segregation of function by providing for family units made up of a mixture of guests, single people, couples, families, older and younger people, all living and working together.

Max

We're designing a number of
family "cells" in which every
function of the community would be
represented. These cells might have
their own sanctuaries, workshops and
alternative energy sources. The idea is
to start with one such unit, learn from
its mistakes, and maybe in a year's
time build a second. This way we can
build organically.

Greta

100   *We have a choice: Do we want to remain a viable evolutionary force, or not? That requires daring. When we reach a point of complexity as we have done, it requires faith to make the next jump — but this is a quantum universe. Evolution is progressing by quantum leaps, and each one of us is required to make all these quantum jumps ourselves. If we don't, we'll end up like any other ivory-towered university, where everything is routinized and the people are processed and stereotyped and bureaucratized; or just a commune, with lots of mental and political discussions and emotions flowing around and around; or an old type of mystery school with rigidities and spiritual dogma and glamorous astral images of the spiritual world that have nothing to do with simplicity, integrity and holiness.*

François

meditation-blessing Newbold House

Many spiritual groups and
movements start with the visionary,
and after a while they reach a point of
stasis; the fear of exploration and the
fear of daring set in. There are
communities and groups which will
stay stuck — they are the ones that are
becoming belief systems: they know
exactly what is the truth and what
isn't, and they mass-produce their
graduates so that they all look the
same; they all have the same words.
Those communities that will be
moving creatively into the next
decade are those which consciously
choose to be flexible and open and to
move beyond their self-definitions.
            Milenko

The New Jerusalem is an all-embracing city encompassing all the nations and cities, religions and tribes, families and individuals that humans create and express within. The New Jerusalem is without boundaries. It has no geographical connotations. Instead, it is a city of the spirit built upon a vision and a definition of the human condition which sees humanity as multi-dimensional and cosmic in its scope. It sees us as being linked not only with all the different aspects of our own beings, but also with the many streams and flows of evolution other than our own.

The New Jerusalem is, in a sense, the city without limits. It is that state of oneness where humans express their basic sense of belonging and of security. Whether physically with people or not, whether living in the country or in the city, no matter where the human is in dimensional Earth, he or she knows the homeland and the freedom of non-dimensionality.

There are those who are the architects of this city, and those who will build it for humanity. Their destiny is to leave the cities of our present consciousness and to build for us the new.

David Spangler

Six or seven years ago, sitting here in a community meeting, there'd be about ninety people. If anyone had suggested that we'd soon top three hundred, many of us might have doubted that an organism such as this could grow in quality as well as in size. In my own life, I've learned not to worry about the future, and I just take the next step and try to apply my efforts to it totally. Having done that, I feel I experience more openness now than I did when there were ninety people here. I don't think we should be frightened of growth and I don't think we should take our visions of it too literally. Whatever form, if any, a city of Light may take, I'm sure it's not going to look like Chicago.

Sheila

Manifestation, Finance, and Right Livelihood

Peter: *In the beginning of 1970, there were only ten people in the community, so we were really surprised when Eileen received guidance one day that we were to build a community center with a kitchen and dining room to serve 200 people. It didn't make sense. Why should we build a community center for 200 when we were only ten in number? We had no money, but we went ahead in faith, and all our needs were met. The right people and the right materials manifested in perfect timing. The community center was completed in six weeks. That year the community grew from ten to forty-five people, and we had hundreds of visitors. We would never have been able to accommodate these people had we not manifested that building by going ahead in faith. Within a year the community had outgrown the dining room and we had to add on an extension.*

Jeremy: Findhorn was built on the premise "Seek ye first the Kingdom of God and all else shall be added unto you." Stories of Findhorn's origin abound with examples of this principle in action. Yet behind the apparent effortlessness of the "miracles" of those early days lay years of hard training and experience in what David Spangler has called the Laws of Manifestation. To master these principles as a community requires us first to master them as individuals, and in this process members joining the community find some of their greatest lessons.

Manifestation is a process of working with natural principles and laws in order to translate energy from one level of reality to another. It is not the creation of something out of nothing, but rather a process of releasing a potential of something that already exists.

Heat is potential within coal. Health is potential within illness. Abundance is potential within poverty. Divinity is potential within humanity.

Manifestation is not a highly esoteric process. It is something we do all the time through our thinking, our feeling, our actions, our very living. We are always manifesting. Understanding this can help us to be manifestors of that which we really want within our lives and the life of our world. David Spangler

For many years at Findhorn, the Laws of Manifestation were expressed as follows:

1. One can discriminate between personal desire and true need by seeking a clear vision of the will of God.

2. One must have a precise vision or idea of what is to be manifested, if necessary sharing that vision so that all who are involved in the process are united in thought and imagination.

3. Ask only once, knowing that in faith the need is being perfectly met. Give thanks that this is so, and then release it from your mind.

4. If action is required, go ahead in faith, keeping in mind the positive thought and image that the need is being perfectly met.

5. When the manifestation occurs, give thanks again. Realize that what you have manifested is not your possession but is an aspect of God placed under your care and trust. Treat all you have with love and skill, recognizing it as a gift from God.

There is no question that the Laws of Manifestation, applied in this fashion, work. The principles involved are largely positive thought and the precise formation of mental images with the consequent concentration of energy, faith and the bridging principle of putting God's will first.

However, using this approach, the individual remains within a subject-object relationship with his world. He is consequently invoking things which are external to himself, the presence of which he does not
104 *recognize within his being or environment and which therefore constitute a lack or need. He is working with God as Principle, yet still in some way as a source external to himself. He is asking for things, acting as a center to which they can be attracted, rather than being the essence of all things and acting as a center of evocation through which the Wholeness (that essence) can externalize itself into appropriate forms. He is trying to draw something from God, rather than working with God to give something new form and expression.* David Spangler

Michael S.: *For me, manifestation has involved learning to expand my awareness. Formerly when I worked at a job, whatever I received from it remained limited, a fixed monetary return I could depend on. At Findhorn I have had to learn that I was working for God – and that there was no limit on the return, no single source of remuneration. I once needed a guitar, for example, and when someone offered to buy me one I had the hardest time accepting it. I felt that it would have been easier to go out and get a job, to earn the money and buy it myself. My lesson was to realize that by directing my energy towards one point – God – my needs are being met at another level. Living in the faith that it works this way means learning to accept it when it does.*

Every member's livelihood is unique. Beyond food, accommodation and staple needs, which are provided by the community, it is up to the individual to take care of one's own well-being, attune to one's own needs, in relation to the whole. Some join the community with money enough not only to cover their membership fees

for a year, but also to ensure a comfortable standard of living for the duration of their stay; others join with little or no money to begin with, though this is not encouraged. For those who are unable to continue providing for themselves, a five-pounds-a-week allowance is available from community funds.

I think if you want a good experience of the Laws of Manifestation then you should get into a meditative state, a highly reflective state – and go hitchhiking

Michael

There is a Sufi saying which goes, "Trust God – and tether your camel." It is a reminder that spiritual principles come into effect only through our own endeavors to accomplish a particular task. Once Findhorn outgrew the caravan park and began expanding the range of its activities, matters of finance and communication became increasingly complex; yet at first there was a curious reluctance to introduce management systems with which to cope, as if they would somehow block the process of manifestation.

Doug: *When I joined the community in 1974 I went to work in the accounts department, and in those days the attitude towards money was very loose. There was no budgeting, no record of payments, and no* figures were ever shared with the community. We knew little about how much money we had or who was spending what. Then when work began on the Universal Hall we found we were £20,000 short, and this forced us to produce our first budget. The fact emerged that a lot was being spent carelessly, and to counteract this we formed our first management group.

This group faced several challenges. Many of its members were former businessmen with a tendency to revert to old techniques which paid little heed to the importance of intuition; when the pressure of their work became overwhelming, their response was often to come down with tighter controls. Also, by isolating the management of the community in a group apart from the working departments, it was difficult to keep members in touch with the overall financial picture, which sometimes resulted in overspending due to a misunderstanding of the Laws of Manifestation.

Michael: *In any community whose members strive towards higher consciousness, the less management the better. It should be necessary only as a point of synthesis, of co-ordination and information exchange. We're still working towards that; meanwhile, if we're not careful, management can fall back into what one could call older patterns of control. In another sense the community is highly unmanageable, because often members have difficulty in that area – they don't like someone else telling them what to do. That in itself is a learning process, as it challenges us to come to terms with a sense of our own personal authority, power and responsibility.*

Final financial responsibility within the community rests with the trustees of the Findhorn Foundation, a small group of resident and non-resident members who are legally bound to ensure that the business and running of the community proceed in a "reasonable" manner.

Ross: *Shortly after we became a charitable trust, the trustees recognized that the ordinary conventions of trusteeship were not applicable to a structure that relied more on spiritual than practical considerations for its development. Thus our trusteeship has become a real adventure in co-creation with the rest of the community. We find that while legal requirements oblige us to see that the funds of the Foundation are used to further the objectives of the Trust deed, we must interpret this to mean that finance be employed to generate and circulate "love in action". This is concerned with giving, not getting; supply, and not demand.*

As we continue to explore and to work with the Laws of Manifestation, we know that there are challenges and pitfalls ahead, but looking back along the path we have already travelled we realize that these are there to help us grow. The measure of our abundance is often seen as a reflection of the consciousness of the community, and those times in which we have experienced financial difficulties have served to generate close examination of how much we are giving out to the world, on whatever level of expression.

In essence, the clue to Manifestation lies in the recognition that God or Absolute Wholeness is the only reality. Thus, everything in the universe is directly or indirectly related to everything else through this Wholeness: and there is no barrier or impediment of time, space or circumstance which can obstruct the right flow of energy between affinities within the Whole. As I think in my heart, so I am; as I am, so I create my world, attract my environment, manifest my Being in relationship to the Whole. God is all there is. In God there is no lack. The more we can perceive and understand this reality and live within it, the more we can work with the Laws of Manifestation successfully on every level and in every circumstance of life.
David Spangler

Giles: Although I was relatively prosperous as an economist before coming to Findhorn, my relationship to the world was fundamentally based on ideas of scarcity. What changed my whole life was the experience of living in Indonesia for three years as an economic advisor. I came to see that the Western ideal of economic development is not only condescending but false. I could see that the culture I encountered in this so-called "underdeveloped" part of the world was far more developed than my own in spiritual terms.

In Java there are over ninety million people living on an island the size of England. The Javanese live almost exclusively on a staple of rice, which they either have to grow or import at world market prices. They treat the rice with great respect, growing it in a process of attunement to the nature spirits, and harvesting it by hand with apologies to the goddess of rice and an explanation of their need. Everything the Javanese do is based on spiritual principles, although they don't think of them as such; they think of them as life-ideas. I could see that the social and economic implications of these ideas were healthier than anything I had to offer. For instance, if you don't use machines to cut the rice, you need the whole village to cut it, and everybody in the village is given a share of the crop for doing that, so there is equal distribution immediately; whereas if you have combine harvesting, the man who owns the machines controls the crop. I was also impressed with the way that villages are run essentially by attunement, through village councils that don't debate issues but speak about them from many perspectives, as we do at Findhorn in community meetings, and come to a consensus in which everybody has participated.

I left Indonesia feeling profoundly changed in my attitudes, and when I came home to England I wasn't at all clear as to what I was going to do, so I went back to an old love of mine, which was building boats. Eventually I came to Scotland looking for a boat-building job, but discovered Findhorn, and ended up staying.

I spent my first six months here as a plumber, then I was asked if I'd like to focalize the small grocery shop that the community runs for the caravan park. The experience of working in the shop was a real course in the principles of manifestation. I arrived on the scene at the beginning of the summer peak period, when suddenly the number of, say, bottles of milk that are sold per day goes from 20 to nearly 400. The shop was short-staffed and the group was putting out the message to the whole community: "Help, the summer crunch is coming and we need people." There was a feeling of panic about the plea, and the community was being told, "It's your duty to help run the shop." Needless to say, the appeal drew no one. So when I arrived, we decided as a crew that we would stop putting out appeals and just get on with the work and enjoy ourselves. Within a week or two the work seemed effortless, and we were fully staffed. At the end of the year the profit for the shop reflected our positive energy flow. For the previous two years the shop had been running between break-even

it says "be still, turn within, know that all is very very well"

Giles Chitty

and a thousand pounds profit. That year there was a profit of over ten thousand pounds. I was quite staggered! It made no sense financially. I couldn't understand where the extra money came from – the turnover wasn't that much greater and it had not been a particularly spectacular summer. In the end the lesson for me was, first and foremost, to do what's right in front of you as perfectly as you can and enjoy it. That, for me, has been the key to manifestation.

As a community, we seem recently to have lost sight of that simple truth. We've expanded all over the place into houses and programs and projects while spreading our consciousness too thinly. We've always said it's our principle to finish thoroughly and perfectly what we start before moving on to anything else. As far as I can see, we haven't lived up to that very often in the last three years. I'm sure this is why we've precipitated a financial crisis for ourselves, and we're having to sell at least one house; not just to pay off our debts, but to draw our spiritual energy into a clearer focus and infuse it in the other forms whose custodianship we've neglected.

In the year or more since I left the shop and have been working with the community's finances, I've discovered that growth has to come from a balance of two kinds of impulse. One is a strong vision, held clearly in our consciousness, which we move towards purposefully, and the other one is that the growth and movement towards that vision come out of love and care for whatever we are having to deal with right now. You need to nurture and love and care for a garden for it to thrive. It helps to have a vision for the garden, but vision alone is useless unless you're prepared to put love and care into each spadeful of soil you dig.

I feel that, at worst, what we've done as a community in Peter's era is to hold a spiritual vision very strongly and in very specific material form and make it happen. That kind of energy flow is a reflection of management patterns in the larger society around us. However, I think that an important difference between Findhorn and the larger society is that we are committed to being flexible in relation to our plans, and we know that there is a divine pattern unfolding throughout the universe which we can sometimes glimpse clearly in part and sometimes not clearly at all. We've learned that we always need to be careful about laying down our own blueprint and then sticking to it just because it's there. It's so easy to become attached to one particular interpretation of a vision, and it's a dangerous thing if we can't release our interpretation as new guidance, or new attunement, or new intuitive feelings come up about the right thing to do now. And guidance isn't always justifiable or completely "reasonable". If Peter and Eileen had always acted reasonably, the community would never have been founded.

Ideally in the New Age, "No management is good management", because we should all be co-creating through universal attunement to the will of God. We're not there yet, but I think we're creating a culture that's cohesive enough and open enough to accept and synthesize what we need to learn without selling out to manipulative solutions. In that respect I feel we're like the villagers in Bali in whose traditional dances there are now Tango steps. They got these from Dutch tourists in the 1930s, but they weren't seduced into switching to the Tango; they took what spoke to their hearts and incorporated it into some of their own dance forms.

III Co-creation

Y ou are in the world of action
where we are not physically embodied, and that is
your great opportunity and privilege.
You are the outer extension of ourselves
as we are the inner extensions of you . . .

. . . When you come to us we would not keep you
but would pass you on in consciousness to the One
of whom we are ever conscious, who is our Life
and the Light of the World.

The Devas

HERE LIES
IONA

SOUND of
IONA

Eileen
Ghomain

Seal
Bay

Skerryvore
Lighthouse
(31 mi.)

Eileen
Dubh

Tinker's Hole

Pigeon
Cave

Hanging
Rock

Dubh
Artach
Lighthouse
(14 mi.)

Eileen Na Muc

Otter Bay

Rankin's Rocks

ISLE of ERRAID
Mull, Argyll, SCOTLAND

RRAID
OUND

Fidden Jetty

Ross of Mull

Telegraph Island

Pier

Seaweed Bay

Ruin

Quarry

Village

Croft

Old Fort

Cnoc Mor

Knock-
vologan

The Narrows

Haunting Valley

Peat
Mosses

e Door

Fairy Glen

The Caribbean

Eileen Dubh

Erraid

E*rray –*
Namit by the Erische (Gaels)
Ellan Erray, ane iyle of
halffe myle lange
and halffe myle braid,
guid main land, inhabit and
manurit, fruitful of corne
and pastorage,
with abundance of fisching.

Donald Monro 1549
Description of the Western Isles

112

Iona's geographical position . . . can be effectively realised on the spot by a survey of the wide and splendid view from the northern hill of the island. It lies in the midst of the Hebrides, or the Western Isles of Scotland, and these varied islands, far and near, great and small, with their vast enchanting setting of ocean and sky, compose the whole of the prospect . . .

To the south-east the three rounded mountains rising side by side above the low line of the Ross are the Paps of Jura, thirty miles away. Islay is next to Jura, and Colonsay in front. The Ross itself ends with Erraid Isle, on which is seen the lighthouse station for Dubh Iarteach and Skerryvore Lights, and off Erraid a high outlying rock islet, Eilean nam Muc, stands sentinel over the southern entrance to the Sound, with the Torran Rocks beyond. Dubh Iarteach is a lighthouse perched on a solitary rock twelve miles south-south-west of Iona, and from it to Tiree nothing breaks the sweep of the sea-line.

E. C. Trenholme
The Story of Iona

Angus: In January, 1978, the Findhorn community was offered the custodianship of Erraid, a small island off the west coast of Scotland between Mull and the sacred Isle of Iona. From time immemorial, Iona has been a place of spiritual power. During the Dark Ages, the light of Christianity was kept aflame there in a very pure form and was radiated out to the world by Saint Columba and his monks. The community is also joint custodian of a small house on Iona which serves as a place of meditation and study, a vital complement to active community life. Erraid is within the aura of Iona but it doesn't have the connections with the past that Iona has, so it offers the foundations for a fresh start in building a spiritual environment.

The houses we live in now were built between 1867 and 1871 by the Northern Lighthouse Company. There is good rock on the island, and they had need of it to build lighthouses, so they built a series of nine cottages and outbuildings within about five acres of walled gardens as a base for lighthouse keepers. Robert Louis Stevenson, author of *Treasure Island*, stayed in one of the houses when he was young. His father was an architect and site engineer for Northern Lights. The cottages themselves are as strong as lighthouses and as beautifully built. The roofs are still as straight as the day they were put up. At the height of the company's activities, over a hundred people lived on Erraid.

Since the fifties, Erraid has been in private ownership and the houses used only as summer cottages. One visionary old lady named Ella Horsey did live there all the year around and later wrote a book about the island.

In 1976, Henk Van der Sluis, a Dutchman, bought Erraid and offered the Findhorn community custodianship of the island provided he and his family could use it for one month each year during their summer holidays.

To start with, four of us went out from Findhorn. We'd all been in the community for at least two years, Holger and myself had been at Findhorn even longer, and Jonathan Caddy had been in the

It's a very intense situation: a small group on a square mile of island.

There are no trees, no cover; you can't hide anything.

Jonathan

113

Angus Marland

community all his life in a sense. We thought that between us we had enough experience to form a cohesive group quite easily. However, we soon found ourselves going through our own form of purgatory in facing up to the difficulties of starting a small community. In the process of establishing a sound group identity in a new environment, we all have had to work on some form of emotional, authority or personal relationship challenge. Fortunately we'd had the opportunity to learn to deal with some of the difficulties that did come up. That's where our Findhorn training came in; it didn't reduce the amount of stuff we had to go through, but it facilitated our working out much of it. The island itself has a tremendous purity and tranquility, and it seems to demand the same of us – anything that isn't aligned to those qualities has been very soon exposed and stripped away.

It was an intense year, but a lot of the groundwork has been done, and I think that from now on it'll be a lot easier. Our major challenges have been to agree as a group to a satisfactory division of responsibilities and to accept the importance of grounding ourselves as a group in attunement and meditation, rather than dealing piecemeal with an isolating, demanding environment. The people who live on Erraid now have had the experience of being taken down to ground level, to foundation level, in the same way that Peter, Eileen and Dorothy had been when starting Findhorn, so that they now have a strong enough base to deal with whatever comes up on the island.

My decision to go to Erraid was part of a desire to see a farm at Findhorn, and Erraid was a step towards that; it was an opportunity to garden a larger piece of ground. So I did that, and I knew that when I went it was only for a year. Now I'm back to working on the land at Cullerne, which I feel is another step towards farming for the community.

I came back to Findhorn from Erraid with considerable objectivity and I still have that, thank goodness. I think the community is going through another major change, as usual; what with the great expansion we've gone through recently and our difficult financial situation, the community could get a little wobbly. So I'm glad that I can come back and contribute what stability I have. And I see it as a stability which was enhanced by my experience of Erraid, which comes from the earth, from the experience of depth and rootedness that working with earth gives.

View of the village and Mull

I wanted to simplify my life and get down to fundamentals. But I found I got more than I had bargained for. A degree in Theoretical Ecology didn't help when the goat got sick. I've found that simplicity and purism aren't the same thing; I mean, if the goat's dying, you suddenly don't feel so squeamish about antibiotics.
Jonathan

When Alice and I first came to talk about living on the island, it seemed to us that the four people here had learned to live together by territorializing their jobs. One would take care of the animals, another the gardens, or the housework, or the maintenance work. They could spend a whole day without talking to each other. They gave that as evidence of their attunement, but the arrival of new people threatened their routine of convenient avoidance. The individual boundaries became confused again, and conflicts arose. They didn't like our coming to join them at the time, but they saw that it was right. They said: ''We don't like it, but come.''
Terry

There are many small considerations that are necessary, living on an island like Erraid, which people in more accessible places take for granted. To me, these things are important elements of being in an isolated place like this. For instance, there is a lot of traffic to and fro to the mainland today, and several people need to be rowed back and forth. I find myself thinking: "Oh dear, I've been interrupted again in the middle of doing something, and now I have to go and pick somebody up, or deliver somebody, or whatever."
Alternatively, I can do it in a frame of mind where I go ahead and experience the rowing, how good it is to be out there, how the wind is changing, what's happening with the tide, how the sky looks, and how the water looks. Just being with the moment.

Margaret

God is a working companion here. There was a time when we needed to get the trader into the water. The trader is a large boat, which it usually requires at least three people to move. Yet there was a time when that trader needed to be in the water, and there was only myself to pull it in. And it got in. I believe that God was pulling that boat with me. I don't believe that I could go down there right now and move that boat. Because there would be no need. But when the need is there, He's there. He is so close. He is just like a working friend.

Holger

118

Part of our vision is that, although we're working towards an understanding of self-sufficiency, in no way do we see ourselves as an isolated unit. In fact, Erraid is part of what's called a crofting township – in other words, a group of crofts, or small farms. We work cooperatively with our neighbors on the island of Mull, helping each other with the sheep, the peat, the potatoes, or whatever.

Angus

Mull *itself is like one big community. Everyone knows what everyone else is doing. The islanders make friends slowly. The time scale is altogether different. For instance, the Gibsons, who own a croft, have been there for twenty years on and off, and they're still regarded as newcomers.*
Jonathan

120 **T**he thing I have learned most clearly, living with a small group, is not to try to give up my identity to help the group. You can't give anything if you lose track of who you are, because then you don't have anything left to give. That's why I started to develop my interest in Celtic design. Iona is where the Book of Kells was inspired, and I've always felt the power of those illuminated sacred texts. Most of my inspiration has come from actually being on Erraid, though; from the clarity of outline and the basic rhythms which are so ever-present here. Celtic art seems to trace the same rhythms in a visual form. The interlacing rhythmic lines appeal to our internal sense of the basic rhythms of life that people can identify with; it's something that goes very deep.

Alice

Celtic Card by Alice Rigan

When I came to Erraid there were certain things within me that hadn't yet been tested at Findhorn, certain lessons I hadn't fully learned to the point where they'd become my knowing, rather than just belief. When we first arrived on Erraid, we were trying to find a way for a group to function without a focalizer or a leader figure. We tried, and we failed. In trying and failing, it's become clear to me that in the initial stages at least, there does need to be some person – it could be a different person at different times – who will accept responsibility for the coordinating role in a group. That's one thing Erraid taught me.

Another lesson I learned was about the power of meditation, especially group meditation. In the first year we spent very little time meditating together as a group and we suffered as a consequence. Now, we meditate together and it's a high priority for everybody. Also, when things get difficult, we try to work them out by sharing our personal experience openly, and that works to an extent. But the real clarity comes from our shared meditations.

Holger

I've seen strengths in Maggie here I haven't seen elsewhere: the strength of being happy in adverse conditions; being inundated with a lot of people and being able to remain centered; being able to take the baby across in a rough sea, and remain centered; being able to wash diapers in an empty five-gallon honey bucket and be happy, and not wish to have the conditions better so that she could be happier.

Holger

It's the first time we've felt such a strain in our marriage, living in such a close situation – a tiny group on a tiny island dealing with basic elements, basic stuff. You can't avoid dealing with one person, as you might at Findhorn, by going to the Universal Hall and seeing three hundred others. There's no way you can be anonymous here. You can't retreat, you can't even miss dinner without everyone knowing it. What it comes down to is that you can't avoid being faced with your self. And the island has been uninhabited for so long that it's very pure, kept clean by the wind. Somehow that purity adds to the intensity. It's like a magnifying glass.

Alice

121

124

It seems that one's personal vision for the place is the first thing to go. We've had lots of individual visions, and they all have foundered. The gardeners tried to do certain things and use practices they were familiar with, but the weather on the island would just shatter what they'd done. They have had to learn to do things in the way the island requires.

Terry

I have become aware of what nature is going to do before it happens: whether the tide is moving in or out, what the weather is doing even when I am inside, what time the sun rises and sets. My values have changed: I used to be irritated if it was raining, but on the island the rain became integrated into my life. I have become aware that the earth breathes – in the tides, the moon cycles, the wind. I have become profoundly aware, walking on the island alone, that my presence was frightening to the other living creatures here. Animals and birds would flee as I came near. I have never before felt that kind of sadness. I knew I would have to relate to other kinds of life from a higher consciousness. I became aware of the powerful simplicity of St. Francis or St. Columba. I felt their presence very strongly. Many people seem to experience it here.

Alice

126

The elements —
earth, wind, sea, clouds, sky - are ever with us
in the Western Isles. There are angelic presences
involved with Iona, overlighting the whole
area, who look after us on Erraid, too.
        There's a tremendous radiating power
in the island, deep down in the earth —
a power that can be tapped in meditation
        Angus

There is a very generally entertained idea that to live on an island is to be "out of things" – an assumption that great significance for humanity is more likely to attach itself to big centres of population – to London rather than Eriskay, say. I see no reason for assuming anything of the sort . . . "It is a remarkable fact," writes Th. A. Fischer, "that in the history of the development of the human mind the great spiritual movements did not always proceed from the most famous and the most powerful nations or cities, the so-called centres of intelligence, but, similar to the mighty rivers of the world, had their sources in localities small, hidden and unknown."

(cont'd.)

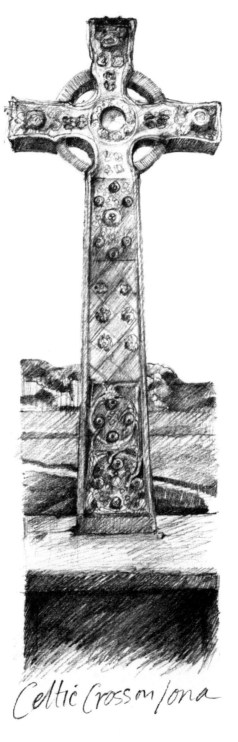

Celtic Cross on Iona

No matter how many millions may be congregated into great cities like London and New York, there is nothing inherently impossible or even improbable in Dr. Johnson's remark that "Perhaps, in the revolutions of the world, Iona may be some time again the instructress of the Western regions," a statement echoing St. Columba's own prediction in the verse which, being translated, reads: "Iona of my heart, Iona of my love! Where now is the chanting of monks, there will be lowing of cattle. But before the world is ended, Iona will be as it was."

Hugh MacDiarmid
The Islands of Scotland

Doves on Iona

Messengers from Within

Yes, I talk with angels, great Beings whose lives infuse and create all of Nature. In another time and culture I might have been cloistered in a convent or a temple, or, less pleasantly, burnt at the stake as a witch. In our skeptical time and culture, such a claim is more likely to be met with scoffing disbelief as the ramblings of a dreamy female. Being a practical, down-to-earth person, I had never set out to learn to talk with angels, nor had I ever imagined that such contact could be possible or useful. Yet, when this communication began to occur, it did so in a way that I could not dispute. Concrete proof developed in the Findhorn garden, which became the basis for the development of the Findhorn Community. The garden was planted on sand in conditions that offered scant hospitality and encouragement for the growth of anything other than hardy Scottish bushes and grasses requiring little moisture or nourishment. However, through my telepathic contact with the angelic Beings who overlight and direct plant growth, specific instructions and spiritual assistance were given. The resulting garden, which came to include even tropical varieties of plants, was so astonishing in its growth and vitality that visiting soil experts and horticulturists were unable to find any explanation for it, and eventually had to accept the unorthodox interpretation of angelic help.

> Dorothy Maclean
> *To Hear the Angels Sing*

Dennis: Findhorn is the unfoldment of a seed planted in 1962 by Peter and Eileen Caddy and Dorothy Maclean. That seed has been nurtured by a number of exceptional people, among them R. Ogilvie Crombie (ROC) and David Spangler, and by thousands more who have given of themselves to its flowering.

The story of the Findhorn garden with its 40-lb. cabbages and other marvels, might have seemed whimsical fantasy were there not growing testimony that something truly extraordinary was happening here.

Professor R. Lindsay Robb of the Soil Association was one of a number of authorities impressed by the vitality and vibrance of the Findhorn garden:

The vigor, health and bloom of the plants in this garden at mid-winter on land which is almost barren, powdery sand cannot be explained by the moderate dressings of compost, nor indeed by the application of any known cultural methods of organic husbandry. There are other factors and they are vital ones.

one of many such letters received by the community

The other factors were Findhorn's co-creation with the angelic and elemental realms.

Both Eastern and Western esoteric traditions hold that all life is an outpost or point of entry through which great intelligences externalize themselves. According to these traditions, devas and elementals are living forces of creative intelligence working behind the scenes. The devic or angelic beings work at that level where the divine image or idea is sketched out into the archetypal patterns for all forms. The devas, whose name stems from a Sanskrit word meaning literally "shining ones", hold these archetypes in consciousness, wielding and patterning the forces which vivify the physical form and stepping these energies down to the elementals or nature spirits, the "blue collar workers'' who build the forms through which Spirit reveals itself. A transmission through David Spangler from a representative of the elemental kingdoms describes their realm and their role:

> *We are not the physical body of the plant but we nurture it and enable it to grow. We are children of the vast reaches of space, as much as citizens of any planet. All that you see, we have formed. We are not simple little beings that appear to flit from flower to flower, or hover about a tree – the simplest elemental of the tiniest flower is still an outpost of vast and cosmic authority. There is no limit to what we can achieve . . . We have access direct to the Solar Logos and cosmic sources beyond. Never underestimate what we are. But we do not have the ability to originate. That is not our function . . . Though we cannot debate human authority, we have the right not to obey, to withdraw . . . Since humanity has not learned to tap its devic essences, such as they are, blended within its human experience, it does not have the same power that we have . . . Hence, nature does not obey humans as swiftly and perfectly as it will obey us.*

The garden blossoming from Findhorn's barren, sandy soil was a spur to our collective imagination – it opened us to the unlimited possibilities of co-creation with the nature kingdoms. We were shown that in cooperation with other orders of being we could work the seemingly miraculous.

There has been an overemphasis, no doubt, on the "magic" of Findhorn. The pendulum has now swung from an emphasis on the magical and enchanted to an emphasis on being divinely ordinary – that is, living an ordinary life in an extraordinary way.

The hallowing of the everyday in a rebirth of wonder – this theme runs like an underground stream through our experience at Findhorn, both

within the garden and without. The recognition gradually begins to dawn that *all* of life is a miracle. In our slumber we have required poets, mystics, children, madmen and other visionaries to point out what was so familiar that we had overlooked it. Emerson said it for us: "If the stars would appear one night in a thousand years, how man would believe and adore."

Luther Burbank demonstrated that extraordinary possibilities are within reach of anyone lovingly and sympathetically attuned to nature. Our work at Findhorn is to nurture this sympathetic attunement through our communion with the devic and elemental realms.

In all things we must be invited into cooperation and communication with you. We cannot intrude . . . Humans must tell us clearly, authoritatively what must be done in full belief of our capacity to do it and in full love of what we represent both as their partners and within themselves. If humans need to do anything, we will inspire them to do it. If something must be added to the soil, we will inspire them to do this, if they open to our inspiration. We have the absolute power to transform the very physical constituency of soil, air, and water without humans having to do anything but inform us what needs to be done . . . There is no limit to

our power, and all forms in nature obey us. But we respond as humans allow us and invite us in love, respect, and deep understanding.

Through the tutelage of David, ROC and Dorothy, Findhorn has been awakened to a renewed consciousness of our affinity with the Being within all form, and thus of our kinship with and responsibility towards all life. Through these three friends, articulate expression has been given to the vision of a united humanity working in harmony with other kingdoms and dimensions of consciousness to create whole beings living lightly on a whole Earth.

Although there is no official canon of beliefs at Findhorn, we recognize, with Thoreau, that "heaven is under our feet as well as over our heads" – that our Earth and its precious cargo of life are sacred.

Just as we are placed in one another's keeping, so too is the Earth in our care. We have been entrusted with evoking from the Earth the fruition of its seed-potential – realizing, making actual, that which was but a promise. In the words of a friend, we help the rose make public what was private in the stone.

As beings learning to grow our godhood together, we see ourselves not simply as creatures, products of God's handiwork, but as co-creators and fellow workers in the unfoldment of a divine process. In this context, spiritual gardening becomes a strategy for discovering our own participatory divinity.

Co-creation with nature ultimately and intimately involves our *own* divine nature. It has to do not just with the greenery we see from our windows, nor simply with our elemental and devic friends behind the scenes. As the devas remind us, there is an aspect of our inner being which is devic. By communing with the devic essence within our own soul, we are ushered into closer contact with trans-human realms, with beings who more wholly embody that fulfilment of which humanity is the seed.

You are on the verge of an absolute breakthrough, a future undreamed of by humanity. Pay heed to my words and know that we extend to you kinship and deeper than kinship, a linking, a marriage, so that . . . a glory greater than humans have known can be made manifest.

We do not wish to present Findhorn's experiment in co-creation with nature either as unique or as an accomplished fact. Rather, it is an area we are exploring, as we begin to bring a new Eden into manifestation in our lives. Yet something about this new world we live in is brought out by saying that the new Eden is both immediate and in prospect; is at once an anticipation *and* a fulfilment accessible now. We are working in concert with many others to bring this vision of a new Earth into manifestation, while bearing in mind that it *is* a vision, and hence just the beginning of responsibilities.

Gardeners meeting

134

Tom: *My love for trees demands from me an intense involvement in any pruning work. I like to watch the tree, often for as much as six months, before I touch it. I take it in from all angles, seeing how its shape and form affects its environment. When the day of judgment comes, I hold it in my thoughts through a moment of silence. During this time of concentrated thought I sometimes experience a heightening of awareness. It's as if in some unseen way the spirit of the tree and I are coming into some vital embrace. This feeling then becomes a warmth, a kind of fire of purpose that directs my work. Detail is demanding—each cut must be clean, exact and smooth against the trunk, which I am as careful not to slip and scar as I would be not to gouge my own skin.*

Adam: *In the vegetable gardens a number of "pests" and diseases appeared. We had rabbits, moles, birds, clubroot on the cabbages, cabbage maggots. We saw it as an opportunity to communicate with other life forms. The gardeners attuned as a group to each organism, and always had positive results. We acknowledged that they had a place, but affirmed that the vision for the garden was to grow food for humans to eat. They were welcome if they could be in harmony with that vision. They stayed, and so did the vegetables. We had beautiful, healthy, vigorous vegetables. We communicated to the rabbits that they were welcome in the garden if they stayed on the grass banks and ate the clover and wildflower there. We asked the moles to leave the garden completely because their presence was too disruptive, but we did suggest an alternative place for them to go. Clubroot (a fungal disease) was on all the brassicas, and yet the plants grew anyway. The prevailing belief is that brassicas with clubroot can't grow into healthy specimens, but our cabbages disproved that.*

Music at Drumduan

135

Rod: *There is a danger, when talking about cooperation with nature, that we perceive it as establishing a relationship with something out there, beyond our four walls. For me, co-creation with nature is the experience of realizing that we* **are** *nature, part of the total balance. Each of us can come to this recognition in different ways. I have the privilege of flying aircraft for a living. Despite their size, speed and power they are still totally dependent on the elements. In flying, just as in sailing, it's the interplay with the elements that brings the sense of oneness. Each time I climb through the clouds or feel the wind buffet my plane, I'm reminded of my place in this beautiful interrelationship.*

Ian: *I left the community for a year after my first stay, when I'd been working in the Findhorn garden. I worked in offices, I sold central heating, I worked in a park, and I found that it really didn't matter what job I was doing because I could get in touch with the same quality of co-creation that I'd experienced in this garden.*

I was sorting filing cards in an office, for instance, and everyone knows that can be a real drag, but when I was prepared to put a bit of life and energy into the job and really put myself in there, it became a totally enjoyable experience. The cards would be working for me, or with me, and I wouldn't have to fumble for them all over the place. It's the same working with a motorcycle or any machinery. If you get in touch with the spirit behind it, it will work with you.

I'd always had a block about Deva messages and the like, but talking with Dorothy I realized that basically I'm guided in action and through action, as though I wouldn't know precisely how to go about something until I picked up a tool and started. There are times when I've had messages, sure, beautifully simple and concise ones. But basically it's only when I get in there and start working with things that I find a kind of response from the environment around me, and it doesn't matter whether I'm plumbing or gardening or making music – it's always there.

136   **B**rian: *When I came to Findhorn in 1971 I began to realize that I was experiencing a broadening of perception; it was as though my physical senses were being extended in a way that's very hard to describe. Walking through the central garden I experienced an extraordinary sense of being greeted and caressed by presences there which seemed to be connected with the flowers. Later that winter I came to follow up that contact with the nature kingdoms when Dorothy asked me to try illustrating her messages from the Devas.*

For me that whole period was like a sensitization process leading me into a whole different area of communication, a way of perceiving too subtle to say it was through images or sound but rather a direct reception of the essence of another being inside my own essence.

I left Findhorn for several years and during the course of that time I rejected that kind of experience as being possibly deceptive. I went into a very fundamentalist Christianity and joined a monastery where such experiences would have been frowned upon anyway.

When I returned to Findhorn, in 1979, it was with a completely neutral attitude to all that I'd experienced previously. I didn't experience the same vibrancy in the garden or any sense of the devic or elemental realms at all.

Then I was invited by a friend over to Newbold House one Saturday morning to meet Harley and Maggie and to see a little grotto they'd found in the garden there that had been hidden for nearly twenty years. As we were walking down a path to see the grotto, I suddenly experienced an overwhelming sense of energy pouring at me from the right-hand side of the path, and sure enough we turned into the grotto which was in precisely that direction.

As we stepped down into the sunken garden, the energy became more and more powerful, and I was left absolutely speechless. I literally couldn't vocalize or use my tongue. I

realized that this wasn't just a residual magnetic energy like you get at a stone circle, but that there was a living presence there, and I had a very good idea of what that presence was. Already knowing the answer I simply put out mentally, "Who are you?", and the answer, which was not a voice – it was more like a total concept fed into my spirit – came back immediately. The nearest I could get to a verbalization of it was simply, "I AM PAN."

That was all really, but I was completely overwhelmed, physically and psychically. Yet it wasn't a threatening experience; it was really uplifting, and it was of a kind with the deepest intuition that I'd had through the Christian experience in the monastery. It was as if I were being shown that there was a continuity, that I didn't have to accept this or that, I could accept this and that.

Michael L.: *For me, getting back to nature isn't so much returning to a state where we grow our own vegetables as it is getting back to our own true divine nature. It's as if I'm focused within the human kingdom at this time, but, as with anything that's focused, like a point of light through a magnifying glass, it always has a broader point of origin. So what I experience as my human existence is very much like sun coming through a magnifying glass, the magnifying glass being my soul. I am a point of pure light on Earth, then, and around that I gather my personality, physical body, etc.*

The point of meditation is to re-establish contact with that part of me not focused within time and space. Because we are also beings of another dimension, of a realm that is not conditioned by time and space, we can, if we have the connections, i.e., the meditative connections, bring through the eternal presence of who we are into any given situation, and thus enhance it.

Lida Sims

L*ida:* Although I once had an experience when I thought I saw a fairy-like face appearing in a cluster of leaves in a huge old oak tree, I really didn't discover much about the subject of the nature forces until some time later when I met a wonderful elderly lady who was well versed in occult and esoteric lore. She told me a great deal about the devic and elemental kingdoms and opened to me her library, which contained many books on the subject.

I was very moved to find confirmation for what in my heart I believed to be true. It accentuated the tendency, acquired as a child, to talk to everything around me. I had grown up in a family accustomed to talking to its dogs, cats and horse, and I had merely extended it to talking to plants, rocks, butterflies and bicycles. I was in the habit of giving them all names and then talking with them. It is something that children often do, to the amusement of the grown-ups around them. At any rate, once again, as an adult, I found myself in the habit of talking with things and plants and animals. Often it would seem that I would get a response, for example, if I was thanking a plant for looking particularly beautiful. Sometimes it would seem to be words, but more often was just a return of energy – a thank you in return or just a feeling of "connectedness" with whoever or whatever it was.

Then I found out about a place in Scotland called Findhorn where people knew about devas and nature spirits and were trying to cooperate with them in their gardening. That bit of information hit me like a shock wave. It was a new step to think about working together with the devas, rather than thinking of them as just folks to talk and listen to. I was so excited that I wrote immediately asking if I could come and visit, though I didn't get there for another two years.

I spent those two years mostly living alone on a small farm. Early in the second spring of my stay, there came one of those very first warm days that makes you sprint outside to get your hands and feet in the dirt. I began working in the garden, and found the day altogether peaceful and joyful. Later in the afternoon, for a rest, I went to sit in a small grove of young white pines next to where I was working. After sitting quietly for a few moments, there crept into my awareness a feeling of agitation and upset. As I had been feeling so mellow I couldn't understand why I would be sensing that. Suddenly I realized it was the trees. It surprised me, and made me realize that the times I had felt a response from plants I talked to were not just my imaginings. I could definitely perceive that the voice had a source other than myself, but could only be picked up within myself. It was a revelation, and what the trees had to say was also a revelation.

They, very much like the faun, Kurmos, that ROC first talked with, could see what humans were up to, but had no way of understanding it unless they were told. What the trees were most concerned about was the fact that I was digging so close to where they were with that noisy, smelly machine (a tiller), and was I going to dig them up as well? Somewhat stunned for a moment, I thought about how humans eat and how trees eat, and told them that unfortunately humans could not take their nourishment directly from the air and earth (as yet, I added), and this made it necessary for us to grow plants which could do so and then to eat them. I told them I was sorry that I had frightened them and had no intention of hurting them. I added that I was delighted to talk

138

to them or anyone else on the farm and would love to try and work with them.

They then seemed to be whispering, passing on what I said from one to the other and commenting on it. The pine grove then seemed satisfied and relaxed, and we sat for a while just enjoying each other's company. I left still feeling a bit stunned, but I knew that contact was possible and had to accept the validity of the experience; I guess the old mind just found it a bit hard to accept.

The next winter I felt changes in the air; I heard more about Findhorn and the work there and felt that it was time to go visit. It was a classic Findhorn story. I went to stay for two weeks and stayed two years. I spent a year in the garden and a year working very closely with people. I went expecting to learn how to talk more intimately with the devas and nature spirits. Other than feeling very much greeted by them when I first arrived, they in fact had very little to say to me. Their presence was always there if I was calm and peaceful and centered, and on rare occasions there would be more specific contact, but for the most part, with the shift in focus of what Findhorn is now about, they kept in the background.

A lot of what Findhorn is about is to see how well you can remain centered, calm and peaceful under circumstances that are divinely engineered to challenge your ability to do so. And so it was for me as I went through that pressure-cooking process that draws one ever closer to the goal of being divinely human – or, as they say in some circles, "enlightened". I learned a lot about being more honest and open with my fellow humans and less about conversing with my fourth-dimensional friends.

I had one very strong experience with the devas which taught me something important. It showed me quite clearly that they welcome human contact, but not only as spectators. It was early in my stay at Findhorn and I was feeling rather low. Here I had come to learn to talk more clearly with the devas, and they seemed farther away than ever. I was thinking how wonderful it was that Dorothy Maclean had taken down all the messages she had received and what a help it had been to me and to other people. It then came to me quite clearly that the devas were interested in people feeling a direct contact with them, and they didn't just want people reading messages through someone else, saying how nice, and not making that same contact themselves. It was clear they wanted me to be able to help others make that contact themselves, rather than do it for them. This would come through a quality of beingness. The process of growth that I would go through at Findhorn would help accomplish this.

I have now left Findhorn and returned to my farm. I have found that the garden is like an old friend who is so new you hardly recognize him. All those plants seem so much more there than they ever were before; but I think it's because I am so much more here than I ever was before. I guess it is not something that they are doing but something that I am becoming that makes the real difference. It's as if I never noticed how beautiful a tomato plant (or anybody else) was before. The reality of it contains all the feelings I had when I was in contact with a deva or nature spirit. But it is just a tomato plant – no frills; just a tomato being itself, and right now for me that's magic.

We call to you, human,
from the highest of our realms, and you are there.
We call to you from densest Earth, and you are there.
We call from other worlds across space, and still
you are there. We are inwardly still attuned, and you share
our oneness. If there are worlds we cannot
reach, no doubt you are there.
"Man, know thyself."

We talk to you from the Kingdom of Nature.
Do not limit the wisdom of that kingdom,
which is the Divine in manifestation and includes obscure
worlds which you disregard at your own peril. You are all things
to all worlds . . . Home in to what you are . . .
Stay put to your immensity.

The Devas

When we ask you to think of plants, or anything,
in terms of living Light, we are not trying to detract
from the beauty of the world as seen
through human eyes, but to add to that beauty,
to add more reality to it, to help you lift all creation.
By thinking in terms of Light you add Light to that already existing;
you speed growth and enhance beauty,
you see truth and link with inner reality . . .

Each individual draws to himself
the result of his thinking . . . Think in terms of Light,
and you will get a response from all creation.
All creation is Light, though obscured by human thought.
Even dense matter will respond, and all will be linked in joy.

Landscape Angel

We thank humanity for planting us so extensively
and enabling us to reclaim much territory. You see, trees are
a protective skin to the Earth and are vital to the planet.
We glory in this; our high praise goes forth like the scent from a flower.
It blesses all who come and rest in our aura. . . .
Trees, rooted guardians of the surface, converters of the higher forces to Earth
through the ground, have a special gift for humanity
in this age of speed, drive, and busy-ness. We are calmness, strength,
endurance, praise and fine attunement . . .
Come to our side whenever you can, and lift your consciousness.

Scots Pine Deva

You come to us and ask
if we have anything to show you today.
Our answer is not to show you anything but to ask that you continually
reach and stay in the state of Lightheartedness,
which is the password to our Kingdom.
Then we can show you what needs to be shown at any time —
then we can be with you in the everyday happenings,
when our practical help would be useful.
We would have our cooperation a constant. We only operate in the present.
We set no store in what has been and while the folklore
of the ages may be about us, we are concerned with what applies now . . .

So when you step out into the day
lift your heart and mind to the Light and keep them there
and we will show you many pertinent things.
Keep relaxed in the Light, and in the moment
we will be present.

The Devas

Yes, I, whom you have contacted,
am concerned with vastly more than your planet,
for I contain or am connected with mineral life which exists
in various stages throughout creation.
Nature is full of paradox, in that as you seek contact with what you consider
a lower form of life, you in fact contact a more universal being.
The mind of man codifies and formulates,
which is within its right and purpose,
but forgets that all is One,
that God is in all, and that the basic substance of life,
which seems most devoid of sensitive consciousness,
is held in its state of existence by its opposite, a vast consciousness,
too vast for you to do more than sense its fringes. . . .

It was the beauty of this particular stone which drew you to me.
Beauty is of God . . . Consciousness of beauty brings you into Oneness,
into any part of the universe.
You are contained in it, just as I seem to contain universes within myself.
The more you appreciate beauty, the more you are linked universally.

Now you feel that you can only look at every pebble
with deepest reverence . . . because you know it is part of my vastness;
and we are glad that in this way
you have been shown a very little of the glory of God –
for the glory of God is everywhere,
stretching from the farthest reaches of all the universes
to the little grain of sand,
one and the same being, held in eternal Love and timeless with Life.

Reverence all life. Emulate my patience.
Unfold the mysteries of God and even of pebbles.
Do it as a learner of life, a revealer.
Let your dominion be over yourself,
and let your expanding consciousness see God's life in all things.
The color and sparkle of a stone is a wonderful thing,
but still more wonderful is the consciousness
which has brought about and brings about these outer manifestations.
Praise God forever, and praise him in the vastness of all life.

Cosmic Angel of Stone

You find in us a power and authority as great
as that of the large trees, although we are the smallest flower
you have contacted. Yes, this is because we are wild, well-established, free
to roam, not dependent on the whims of man.
Of course deva patterns are most clearly imprinted
where plants can root naturally . . .

Understand how related and dependent life is.
Oneness is fact, not theory,
and all life demonstrates this to seeing eyes.
See also the value of contrast . . . You cannot compare us.
Each member of Nature is different and unique. But you humans
spend your lives comparing what you haven't with what others have,
whether it be clothes, gardens, money, views, ailments, time . . .
All you need is to be what you are, to be the unalloyed
pattern of you, and you will draw the right conditions to yourselves.
Then your voice will be just as strong, just as right
as any other voice.

You cannot cease wondering at the power of my voice.
I have found my niche, I am where God means me to be, and therefore I am
as powerful as any in the land. I AM power – I, the synonym for shyness!
Nothing in this world or the next can shake
those who follow their ordained pattern and do God's will unreservedly.
Find and follow God's will for you,
and your voice will be power.

It seems that I must begin and end
on the note of power – God's power, not mine. But I know you love me for
other qualities, and in love I leave you now.

Wild Violet Deva

You are reaching up to the cause of things
and leaving behind the world of effects, which is the sum of man's usual knowledge.
On no account be weighed down by a feeling of ignorance and inadequacy,
because it is this feeling that keeps man in limitation.
You know that there are these vast inner worlds
and you know that you can stretch out to them.
Therefore, cease lamenting and simply leave the old, limiting world.
There is always an invitation to the One World from us.

Landscape Angel

The Universal Hall

In my experience as an architect outside the community, there was always an emphasis on the finished product, while here the emphasis is on the process. We use two approaches which complement each other in designing the building. George and Frances, the two other people I work with, are more in tune with the meditative approach – trying to discover the etheric design – while I'm trying to listen to the needs expressed by the whole community. We work together, though, and I'm very aware of the design coming through a group being. So you couldn't say, "He did this and I did that." There have been occasions when I really felt the flow of Spirit coming through. Most importantly, we agree that we're trying to design an environment that is flexible, conducive to healing, and which allows communication in which people can share from the depths of their being and from the silence.

Roger

The most obviously striking feature of the Universal Hall is that it has five sides. The number five is said to represent the perfection of humanity, the meeting of spirit and form . . .

. . . The inner circle touching the center points of each ringbeam in the Hall is 174.6 feet in circumference. Traditionally in sacred geometry, numbers are highly potent and profound in meaning. Pythagoras and other ancients believed that numbers and figures could represent a true synthesis of knowledge. These abstractions were long used as a language in themselves to communicate cosmic truths beyond verbal description. In alchemy the number 1746 means fusion . . . the combination of celestial and terrestrial forces. . . .

. . . There are many intriguing geometric symbols or correspondences in the Hall. Yet it is important to remember that most of the geometric correlations in the Universal Hall's proportions evolved through an intuitively guided plan rather than through conscious intention. Most ratios, angles and parallels with other sacred structures were discovered after the actual construction.

Marcia

Often we look at this or that area of the building and we talk about what we're learning from it; we start to view the Hall as sacrosanct. Yet I really see that if this building burned down on the day we completed it, the Being of the Hall would go on living, because it's within me and within all of us who have worked on it. All that we've put into it and all that we've learned from building it we're going to carry with us wherever we go.

Timothy

152

We've learned
a lot about how the
life or consciousness
that goes into a
structure
reflects its final
integrity

Lyle: The Universal Hall is to me what the Findhorn garden has been to Peter and Eileen. It has been my teacher for five years. It has been my source of spiritual unfoldment, and it has taught me all the Findhorn lessons: to recognize the life in the materials I'm using, to release myself from attachments, to work with people in a group, and to see a consciousness in the form I'm building.

I'd been working as a professional carpenter and builder in wood for ten years. Coming here slowed me down. That was necessary to change my relationship to the materials we were working with – stone, bricks, timber – and also because our state of consciousness really affected the building. I had to go through a process of transformation. It took me a while to realize it, but I had chosen to do that. Because it slowed us all down and because there were no economic or business pressures, there was inefficiency. I know I don't work at the same pace as I would on a normal construction site. I'm not sure that it's healthy to work at that pace or whether it's valid to use Western business as a yardstick for productivity and accomplishment. I think there is a balance point that we're approaching.

Lyle Schmadt

The Hall was envisioned from the outset as an all-purpose performing arts center and a place for the community to gather. The building itself has evolved as we have become more sensitive to the energy that is contained within the structure. For us this happens to be a very special building but, in another sense, it is no different from any other construction. We've learned a lot about how the life or consciousness that goes into a structure reflects its final integrity. To me it would be ridiculous to hire a regular construction company with aggressive or hostile interrelationships to, say, build a church. You could do it, but you'd just end up with a mere building; whereas, if you have people who are discovering who God is in the process of building, then you have a much more profound space in which to come together as a congregation. In the same way, I feel it's important for families to build their own homes and thereby discover more about how to work together. Then their home actually supports them in being a family.

We had no comprehensive set of plans for the building before we began. When the foundation was being built, all we had clear was the general shape. What we were building was the foundation and the external walls. We designed the rest as we went along. That allowed us to develop a different kind of relationship with the

Ringbeam foundation

154

Richard: *There I was the other day, laying out the dimensions for the new blockwork with George, and Lyle comes up and starts to do it for us. I mean he just kind of took over. So I found myself getting angry and wanted to tell him to get the hell out, but instead I stopped myself and just stood there thinking, "Now we all love each other, right? So how can I tell him how I feel without reacting personally — just speak to him naturally as my brother and not get excited?" So I waited until I was relaxed again and then said, "Lyle, can I make a suggestion?" Lyle looked up and said, "What?" "Could you go find something else to do?"*

Lyle: *You know, when Richard said that to me I was stunned. I didn't know what to say. I kind of backed off sputtering, "But you don't . . . er . . . but I can . . . uh . . ." and I went off to realize what I had been doing, being too much like an overbearing parent and not trusting everybody enough. It was beautiful. Later, during coffee break, I said to Richard, "Next time I do something like that, get angry at me so I can get angry back! The way you did it, I could see myself* **too** *clearly!"*

building. My hope is that, having done that, we can go ahead with other buildings in a clearer way.

At first we worked with professional building contractors, but as we gained confidence and skills we gradually took over. Our attunement and understanding of what we were doing also outgrew the straight professional approach. We expected a lot more of ourselves than simply getting the job done.

Working on the roof was probably the most attuned group experience I've ever known. It had to be. It was dangerous, precise work. Since then, for the most part, it's been more a matter of two or three people, sometimes just one, working to complete different jobs throughout the building. We've had to discover a new way of feeling connected with each other as a group without necessarily working on the same things together. The community as a whole has been going through the same situation in its expansion into a village. It's very easy in this situation, when you lose touch with each person's process, to also lose touch with trusting that person or group of people. Then you have to get together and talk about all the deliberations that have gone into decisions that have been made, and it usually comes down to, "Well, O.K., I can see now why you did that and, even if it was a mistake, I can see what led up to that choice, and it's all right. We can build from it."

It has always seemed, particularly with the roof construction, that we do things the most complicated way possible. For instance, instead of making something perfectly straight for thirty feet, we put an almost imperceptible curve in it to give a lift to the eye. If we'd just built the Hall according to initial plans, we'd have finished it much sooner. But we wouldn't have the building we now have, nor would we have what we've gained, immeasurably, in consciousness.

I was away for a year in 1976 and when I came back people were talking about the building in a way that was new to me. Now, words like "temple" and "the Being of the Hall" would crop up, and people who were psychically sensitive had discovered all sorts of sacred geometric symbols and proportions. They told us that there were five ley lines intersecting in the middle of the building. We became somewhat bogged down because we started to put so much significance on the esoteric and the symbolic that we weren't getting on with the job. We've now come back into balance because

You know, sometimes there's a little tension between Richard and me. Something happens that sets us off. Maybe it's because we both know a lot about building – a little feeling of competition, perhaps. But when we let it out, and share it with each other and the whole group, it's so beautiful. It's like we hold each other in love, and whatever hassle there is becomes a tool we all use to grow. It reminds me of the story I read to my daughter about Eagle, Moose and Bear. You see, Eagle and Bear have a fight going on. Eagle lives up on the mountain, Bear lives down in the forest, and Moose lives between the forest and the mountain. Well, Eagle throws stones down from the mountain at Bear, and Bear throws sticks back from the forest. But they always miss each other and all the stones and sticks land right in front of Moose. So Moose builds a beautiful house with all this material that keeps landing in his front yard. And that's just what this group is doing. Every hassle becomes a way to deepen ourselves, to change, to create something new.

Lyle

155

we have to take care of ourselves here on this earth plane as well; we can't just space out the cosmic reality of what we are doing.

Whenever I come back from being away for a while, I stand back and look at the Hall dispassionately. I look at the stone walls, for instance, and the difference between the professional stonemason's angular perfection and the wall we've built that looks like it's just grown there. It starts out a bit ragged; then, if you look carefully, you can see how people gained the skill as the wall rose upwards. The lasting impression is one of variety of skill and approach, balanced by a sense of rare quality and integrity in the building as a whole. There are areas where things that didn't measure up to our standards had to be taken down and rebuilt. Personally, I know that any time I'm going along doing something and thinking, "Wow, you're really doing this well, Lyle; you're really good at this," any time I get into that space of affirming who I am based on what I can do, then I make some mistake that's in a place where it's totally obvious. And, to correct it I would have to do a lot of work and waste a lot of material. So I just have to say to myself, "O.K. There is a mistake that people will notice, and it will show that this building was built by fallible humans and not according to some faceless professionalism."

Sharing the building with the community has been very exciting: using it for festivals, dances, conferences and the like. I experience it as a totally supportive space. Somehow it puts every performance or sharing that happens there in a much more complete context that we've created.

I feel we've helped Findhorn in this building process through a transition from being a community centered around a garden, with the spiritual lessons learned from cooperating with nature in that way, to working with the theme of cooperation in a more expanded sense. Not only have we expanded our awareness of what it means to cooperate with each other, but we have also co-created with aspects of consciousness and wisdom that transcend this planet and that are here to help and guide us. I know these powers exist, and I've experienced their assistance in my life. I've ceased trying to conceptualize such experiences. I just know that their transformative value in my own life is real, and I have had to learn to work with them.

---

156   *When I first came here it was midsummer, and I found myself working on the roof structure which was being built on the Hall. I felt I was out on the roof of the world, totally exposed and vulnerable. That was how I felt just being in the community. I remember there was a dance during the midsummer festival when the roof was nearly finished, before the structure was covered over. We all danced a Sufi spiral dance together. It was the first time I felt I met the whole community, looking into everyone's eyes as we spiralled past each other. The sense of midsummer timelessness is so strong, especially in these northern latitudes when twilight just merges into morning, that I can't remember if it was then, or on another occasion shortly after, when a rock-and-roll dance moved spontaneously into a free-form meditation. I don't know if it came out of a single flute, or any music at all, but I remember everyone suddenly looking up, in unbroken silence, through the uncovered diamond structure of the roof at one star shining directly above.*
John

It's a wonderful story of synergy.
All the parts of the roof work together.
they all hold each other up. If one
hip falls, the whole structure falls;
but falling is impossible
because they all hold each other in place

Shelley

Construction group watching themselves on video

158

When I came to work on the Hall there must have been about fifteen men in the crew and two or three women. The guys were really open. Underneath the teasing there was a lot of love. As I went through that year-and-a-half, I realized how grateful they were to have women in the Hall. They recognized the need for the balance. The crew gave me lots of support to be a female and not one of the boys. They really taught me the meaning of the word "gentleman". They can be very "macho," heavy-working fellas, and yet there's a real gentleness to them, a soft side that they're willing to share. So working with that many men taught me a lot about my own femininity.

Judy

One of the experiences I'll never forget was being shown how to brush the wooden beams once they had been burned and, as I did so, spending hours in those clouds of soot reflecting on the fact that here we were, putting as much love back into what had grown in the forest as it was possible for us to do. We were letting every single one of those trees, moving into its final resting place, sing its own particular song through all the different twists and turns of the grain and the years' growth rings. And, when you know trees, you can read the whole life of that tree in each wooden beam.

Jeremy B.

Before, when I was earning money, there was always a part of me that wanted to run away, to leave. It wasn't exciting enough. I looked at the people around me and wondered how I could ever go on like that for the rest of my life. I came to Findhorn and worked for ten months on the construction of the publications building. I began working and at some point the resistance started. I thought, "I always work, and feel that I don't want to be doing this. I'd rather be doing something else." But I made the best of it, raised my spirits and finished the job. Later, working on the Hall, I faced the thought, "Could I possibly be happy doing this for the rest of my life?" And suddenly the answer was "Yes", because I believed in what I was doing. It was no longer just a menial task. Now when I am building, it isn't just me being a mason, it is me contributing to something I believe in. And now when I ask myself, "What am I building?" I realize that it is open-ended; it is as big as my concept of myself is. It is infinite. It will keep expanding as I grow with it. What we are building, what we are part of, is a contribution to a new consciousness. The building is only a physical manifestation of that.

Richard

When we think of world service, we tend to think of what we are doing to help world problems such as Ireland and the Middle East. But I am a world problem, you are a world problem, and our neighbors are world problems. The place to solve world problems is within our own consciousness, and then in our immediate affairs. Then, if necessary, the ways will open for us to have conscious, knowing influence over what we call world affairs.

Those individuals who worked on the great cathedrals of the past, knowing they would not live to see their completion, did not allow a sense of personal termination to deter them from the full application of their creative power. The "cathedrals" of the New Age, the temples of transcendent humanity, are being built now. The cornerstones have been laid. We are now in the process of building the superstructure.

The New Age has nothing to do with time. It is a condition of attunement. The "temple" we are building, we are building always. We have been building it for millennia. The few years that we are encased in physical form simply mean that we are working on a different level of the scaffolding. When we leave the physical form, we are still working on the same structure. We are just on a different level.

David Spangler

Haydn Stubbing painting one of two murals for the Hall interior

The Hall itself seems to encourage a receptive state. I've noticed that anyone going in there and trying to take command of the audience usually falls flat. However, if someone is trying to communicate something in a spirit of giving and receptivity, they don't even need to raise their voice to be heard.

Frances

The configuration of the stage area is unusual, and so is the relationship of the performer to the audience. The audience is very close, and it seems the most concentrated audience I've ever performed before. There is a tremendous feedback that comes from a very positive concentration. I feel that everybody is for me, supporting me.

I know that a lot of times it's the professional entertainers who've been most unsettled by such concentration. I can understand that because it has a fantastic stillness. You can almost hear the stillness. In a regular proscenium arch theater you don't see the audience at all. It's a bit like they're out there in the dark looking in through a lighted window which separates and protects you. In the Hall, you are surrounded on three sides, and yet it feels so friendly. The lighting makes a difference; you can't completely isolate the stage area from the audience. They are right there, very much a part of what's happening. Often I felt I would have been quite happy to just stand still, or stop the whole performance and do something over again.

Derek

166 From the time when Bernhard Wosien first introduced sacred dance into the community, these dances have been a great source of inspiration to me. I experience for myself what he means in saying that, when we dance these old forms, it is as though we are entering another time and are guiding ancient knowledge into this present movement.

Though I have had difficulty remembering all the sacred geometric parallels and the spiritual symbolism of the movements, gestures and postures, I can feel the strong energy of creativity and love which the dance generates, a union between dancers on higher levels as we move together. It is a true commun-ity activity. The total experience of sacred dance has brought me into touch with a creative part of myself which I never knew existed. The rhythms of dance are the rhythms of nature, and so my relationship with nature and my work in the garden have also been deeply enriched.

Christopher

François Duquesne

Charles King

When I'm in the Hall, even when 167
it's packed full of people, there is
always a deep well of emptiness and
silence to draw on. It's a quality that
amplifies and resonates through
everything that is communicated
there — especially through joy, music,
laughter, in even the most uproarious
gathering. You can see it in people's
eyes. I think it's that silence that's the
source of the Universal Hall's power
as a tremendous transmitter and
receiver of other ways of being and
thinking and seeing the world.
                    Tim

Al Huang

Candlelight meditation, the Hall

The Network of Light

Marion: I was twelve when I first decided that I wanted to see the world. It was the most powerful impulse in my life. After leaving school I didn't go to university but began travelling instead. In the years since I left my home in Australia I've gradually become aware of how travelling was my education and how, in that sense, the Earth has been my teacher.

When I came to Findhorn with Paul we both had a strong sense of being in the right place at the right time, and we knew within half an hour of arriving that we were definitely going to stay.

My first job in the community was working with mail orders for our publications. I found myself writing to people all over the world, in reply to personal questions and responses that people would send after reading about Findhorn. I began to realize how powerful and universal is the image of the Garden from which this community grew. We even had letters from Russia asking about the garden. Mostly I'd get letters from people who were moving into new areas of consciousness, many of whom would say, "There isn't anyone here with whom I can explore these ideas. It's such an inspiration to know that there are people elsewhere doing what I'm feeling, and that we can connect and share in the same work even though we may be far apart." It was really a very mundane job with lots of book-keeping and routine work. But each day was inspiring; and it was my first insight into the networking in which I have found myself increasingly involved. I felt that every letter was, as Peter puts it, a thread of light in a growing tapestry.

Paul: After working as a stone mason on the Universal Hall for a year, I was asked if I'd like to join the guest department. I'd really enjoyed working with the construction crew and I was inspired by what the Hall symbolizes as a point of aspiration for the community, but basically I'd been happy to take a back seat. My attitude to the world was, essentially: "Let me do my own thing as best I can, leave me alone and we'll get on fine." Suddenly, being asked to join the guest department was directly asking me to participate, to be vulnerable and step out onto the stage and say: "This is what I feel, this is what I think, and this is what I interpret Findhorn to be doing."

It was very challenging, having guests ask me profound questions about the inner workings of Findhorn and on every aspect of our purpose. It really made me stop and take stock of what I was doing and what I actually did feel about being here. So I learned a lot from looking at my life that way. When I would share my perspective with the guests I'd say: "This is my perspective, and if you ask any of the three hundred or so other people who live here you'll get their perspective, and it's not going to be the same as mine." Learning that kind of acceptance of unity in diversity I've found invaluable.

I feel that the experience of visiting Findhorn has been a useful one for thousands of people over the years, but I think there's going to be a shift in emphasis from that aspect of the community's work. What we've been able to offer is an experience of community. We've been offering a safe place for people to open themselves, step beyond some of their own self-imposed boundaries and fears, and reveal their godliness to themselves and to each other in a group context. But far more people throughout the world are creating that sort of context for themselves now, so they don't have to come here

Paul & Marion Stoker

to experience it. It doesn't mean that we'll abandon our workshops and our educational focus, but that we'll be able to explore and share with others our exploration of more specific projects, in greater concentration and depth.

Marion: I found myself increasingly involved with Findhorn's communication with the world at large, through dealing with people who wanted to translate our books, reprint articles or produce films or music from the community. Soon I found myself working with a video-communication project set up by an American group called Karass to link the three communities of Arcosanti in Arizona, Auroville in India, and Findhorn. Through that, Paul and I eventually came to participate in another Karass project, the Hexiad planetary learning team. We joined two people from each of the communities involved in the video link to form a group which spent five months together visiting each of the communities and exploring what we had to share with each other. It was the most intense experience of group consciousness I've ever encountered. We lived and travelled and worked with the same people twenty-four hours a day for five months without a break; there was nowhere to hide any part of ourselves.

Both Auroville and Arcosanti are as different from each other and from Findhorn as are the different continents and desert landscapes in which they're situated. Yet there were times, especially in Auroville, when I felt as if I were at Findhorn. There was something in the people and their relationship to the land itself; maybe it was the sense of an enduring struggle to be fully conscious.

When we'd been on the road for four months and were all gathered in Greenville, New Hampshire, a video letter came from Findhorn. I remember watching it with the group – we'd become very close and knew each other inside-out by then. I just sat there and watched this tape with my head in my hands. It took me back to when I first left Findhorn and how I was so insular without realizing it, in the way I was just parroting things I'd learned; they were a part of me, but I was using jargon that other members of the group didn't understand. I remembered a tape I had made with Peter Caddy. He was being very straight – he had his suit and presentation voice on – and he was saying, "Well, we have to be very aware of how we present ourselves to the world because images have such power over consciousness." I could understand that, and yet somehow our true selves weren't coming through, because it was as if we were busy *presenting* our vision, rather than just being it. That, to me, has been the prime discipline we've been working with – being there, listening with an empty mind, so that we can actually hear what we all have to communicate . . . not just the words, but the essence of the communication.

Paul: I really appreciated Findhorn when we returned from our travels. It's easy to become cynical about the gap between our visions and our struggles while you're here. Yet visiting other communities made me realize how much we have learned, on a social-interaction level, about the basic skills of creating a new society: how we care enough to be with one another and to work through conflicts and really tackle our differences and problems, instead of suppressing them or letting them lie. And I think there has been a real shift in the four years since I came to Findhorn, from the somewhat enclosed focus in which we've been learning these lessons of community to a more expanded sense of planetary communion in which we each take responsibility for co-creating a whole Earth, individually, together and with all the kingdoms of life.

Auroville

Arcosanti

Greenville, N.H.

Ralph: Scattered around the Earth are untold thousands of individuals, small groups and communities quietly creating a society based upon the unity of the human family and co-creation with the forces of nature. Part of our work at Findhorn is to link with a wide range of these centers, organizations and individuals to reveal an emerging pattern that we call the "network of Light".

Although visionary groups have appeared in past centuries, they are now forming on an unprecedented scale. Many of these centers are developing wholistic new patterns of relationship, education, government and technology which may prove vital to the survival and transformation of humankind and the development of a new civilization. Increasingly we're seeing that each group's vision is a facet in the emergence of a collective new image of planetary humanity.

Findhorn's involvement in the network of Light is as old as the community itself. Peter was introduced into the work in 1945 when he was in the Royal Air Force on a visit to the Far East.

Peter: *The evening before I left Singapore for Japan, an officer told me to call upon a couple at Clark Field, an American airbase in the Philippines. When we landed I went 'round there and a rather elderly woman, the mother-in-law, answered the door and invited me in. She offered me a drink and we started talking about Tibet and then the Age of Aquarius, the Age of Woman and the Tibetan.*

She told me about the network of Light. She was the focal point for a group whose work had been to locate centers of Light throughout the world and to link them up telepathically. Eventually Naomi, as she was called, came to Findhorn to be one of its founders. Our early work here for three or four years was entirely on the inner planes, linking up through meditation and

tuning in to these centers twice a day; receiving visions and telepathic transmissions until we had files of information on the 370 centers with which we connected.

A few years ago we were told it was time for these links to be brought down into the outer world. Physical connections had to be made after the inner links had been formed.

The first steps in this direction were taken when Peter and Eileen and other community members went on tour, giving presentations in various countries about the life and vision of Findhorn and the New Age. These events brought together all sorts of people, often from spiritual or new age groups based in the same area that had not previously initiated contact with each other. In this way Findhorn could serve as an agent of synthesis.

Helen: *The challenge of the future is to reach out to embrace all groups that are working in a way that benefits humanity, regardless of labels. That's where courage comes in — to really step out and be open to people on different paths who may even have initially hostile or critical attitudes to what you are doing.*

The creation of a guest program in the community in 1974 has enabled Findhorn to establish connections with people from all over the world. During the summer it is usual for as many as a hundred and fifty guests to be present in the community each week. Nearly 4,000 guests come a year. They represent a wide spectrum of nationalities, ages and professions.

Working in the guest program as a group focalizer, as I have done, is to experience planetary consciousness and the network of Light not as abstract concepts but as part of one's daily

life. One comes to know and feel that a massive transformation is taking place throughout the world. Far from being a fringe phenomenon limited to the youth of a few countries, the shift of consciousness is evident in the people of all ages who come here from all quarters of society, from university professors to industrial workers.

 173

The major emphasis in Findhorn's work during the latter part of the seventies and into the eighties has been to facilitate this process of global transformation. Numerous workshops and yearly Onearth Gatherings provide a dogma-free exploratory setting for people from different paths to come together and meet synergistically.

In the early seventies our knowledge of groups involved in explorations similar to our own was relatively small. Our system of network information storage consisted of a crude card-file in a shoe-box on Peter's desk. We now have a communications center with files listing over 6,000 individuals, groups and communities with whom we have had contact. The files include groups working in a range of activities and disciplines – alternative technology, wholistic healing, new psychologies, new age politics and education, traditional and esoteric spiritual paths.

Some of the information is now being transferred to a micro-computer to facilitate storage and retrieval. This computer in turn is linked with a computer network called Electronic Information Exchange Service (E.I.E.S.), which permits instant communication between a growing number of places on the planet – where terminals are linked through the international telephone system. The advent of computer conferencing has considerable potential for accelerating human evolution through increasing the rate and range of interactive feedback.

More and more of us seem to be learning that there is no threat, no hidden incrimination for us in another person's path. I do not think we are being invited to lose our identities in the process of networking. Rather, I think we are being challenged to grow larger in our knowledge of who we really are. We can each play solo, but we are being asked to play in concert with one another.   Bill Becker

There are many networks, from the telepathic to the electronic, and linking in Spirit continues to be a vital aspect of our work. At sanctuary gatherings and in smaller groups we continue to radiate light and love to many points and individuals throughout the world by visualizing our interconnected energy fields in meditation. One of the community's strongest inner links is the triangle of Light we visualize between Findhorn, Iona and Glastonbury, which connects us with a stream of energy associated with the source of Celtic Christianity and the Grail legend. For the network is not an exclusively human affair: it is also an etheric phenomenon.

Astrophysics tells of different kinds of fields of energy and radiation that envelop our Earth. What we call the etheric body of the Earth is such a field, an aura of energy which gives vitality to the physical body of the planet. The Earth is surrounded by its etheric field or vital body which can receive energies from higher dimensions of vibration, and transform these energies into qualities capable of nourishing and vitalizing the denser matter of the physical level. The etheric field, then, is the source of the primal creative energy from which forms are built, and from which they are sustained in their being. The optimum way for these energies to enter into the physical life-stream of this planet is through the gateway of human consciousness.

David Spangler

. . . Etheric energy may actually be coming very close to empirical verification. Neuro-anatomists have noticed that the electrical paths of the nerves seem to develop before the actual growth and development of the nerve tissue itself. This apriorism of form and pattern over matter absolutely refutes our simplistic notions of mechanism and behaviorism. These proto-neuronal pathways, then, seem to be something like ferro-magnetic domains that can give orientation to the energies flowing through them and actually help to build up the nerve tissues that will grow within the domain pathways. It may now very well be the case that the Kirlian photography of the auras and energies flowing out of the bodies of animals and plants . . . may be images of the etheric energy of the body. According to Spangler, this energy is not "simply located" in the body; the individual body is a prehension of the etheric field around earth.   William Irwin Thompson
Passages About Earth

The connections between the etheric and the physical, the visionary and the substantial are currently being explored in many ways. The Hexiad experiment is the most structured attempt to link new age communities that were first perceived as connected on inner levels.

Arcosanti is a project in the Arizona desert to create a model city based on the principles of new technology and ecology which harness the sun as the main provider of energy and food. Auroville, in India, is a spiritual community which seeks to synthesize Eastern and Western cultures and provide a model of practical living and inspiration for the Third World.

The Tor - Glastonbury, England

The evolutionary spiral teaches us that crisis precedes transformation. For most people the crisis in world affairs is more obvious than the signs of transformation. The mass media tend to amplify dissension, breakdown and destruction and do not balance it sufficiently with reports of breakthrough, creativity and newness. What we therefore need to create, and are creating, is an alternative communications system – to pick up and amplify and see the relationship between the growing responses to crisis.
Barbara Marx Hubbard

175

The Hexiad Project began in 1974 on a level of personal visits to these centers. Later, equipment was provided for video letters to be sent between them. In 1978 it was decided to create a "planetary learning team" in which members from each of the communities participated. By recognizing that individual differences are assets, not liabilities, Hexiad did develop channels of communication for sharing skills, experience, vision and goals, and is currently seeking to understand how these awarenesses can best be shared outside the circle.

Hexiad participants speak of having their experience of family extended beyond their own individual communities. Findhorn itself is now an extended family maintaining contact in various ways with over 400 extended members throughout the world. As we have grown as a family and a community we have come increasingly to know ourselves as part of a pervasive process of planetary transformation, not just through messages received in the inner silence, but also through practical participation in the lives of thousands of individuals and groups.

Yet the network of Light is more than an alternative communications system. We stand between the Earth and the stars, on the threshold of a transplanetary destiny. As we move into the last two decades of this century, the network of Light is simply another image for an evolutionary convergence of consciousness, Earthkind's coming of age. Wherever there are people with an understanding of the unity of all life, whether they are relatively isolated individuals in the midst of industrial civilization or members of a new age community, there stands a point in the network. Ultimately we are moving towards a time when the network of Light becomes so complex and interrelated, so intricate that finally there is no network, there is just a planet of Light.

Afterword

When you read the Findhorn story, it is important to realize that what you are reading is a truly universal story, a timeless one, although a personal story to each. When people first come to Findhorn, they undergo the various challenges that arise from learning to adapt their life to a new place, new rhythms of working and new people. After a while, Findhorn becomes less a place, and more a quality of consciousness. People no longer feel tied to this center in Scotland, but truly feel themselves part of a universal community, and know that the principles in action at Findhorn are applicable anywhere.

This awareness does not come simply from living at Findhorn, but because individuals have learned to see in clearer perspective. They have begun to see that the evolution of the human spirit and the various challenges involved are something in which we all partake, wherever we are, whatever we are doing. With that realization, one knows that one is part of the new world being born, and will always be part of it, and can contribute to it even in the most apparently limiting conditions of life.

We are asked to develop a universal consciousness. Questions such as, "Is Findhorn really the way I want to go, or is another center better for me?" are not relevant. The way towards universal consciousness cannot be represented solely by any one center. If there can arise a significant number of human beings who can draw directly upon the divine impulse within themselves and hence draw directly upon the incredible resources of the super-sensible realms, then we have the capacity for transforming this planet.

People say, "What can *I* do? I am just a single individual." But as a single individual you are still a point of God creativity. You are either manufacturing darkness through your own inner states of anxiety and fear and separation, or you are creating light and revelation through your abandonment of those past states and your attunement to new ones. The world offers us much to be pessimistic about, but that which is within us offers even greater material for creative optimism.

Many people see Findhorn as a place; but to understand truly what Findhorn is seeking to make manifest we must see it from the inside out, and that means from the center of our being outwards. This is true of any of the other centers of Light that are now beginning to emerge. New age communities are springing up in many countries, and small groups of people are coming together to help educate each other into a new way of living. All of these people are agents of the divine plan, in order that at this time in human history there might be worldwide demonstrations of the birth of a new Earth and a new humanity.

World transformation is something that anyone can be involved in, anywhere. The New Age is too vast to be contained within a single structure, person or group. We need only to ask ourselves, "Am I being a way? Am I simply being a satellite in orbit around fixed ideas, or a new sun giving forth my own light of revelation? What am I doing to transform myself and my world?" As we confront these questions daily in our living we will be the revelation of the answers and the creators of a world made new.

So the message of Findhorn, the message which is unfolding throughout the Earth, is for humanity to awake, to arise, and to *be* the creators, now, of the world you have envisioned, and through envisioning are bringing into being.

David Spangler